The short course in

BEER

Author of *The New Short Course in Wine*

LYNN HOFFMAN

The short course in

BEER

Author of *The New Short Course in Wine*

LYNN HOFFMAN

CLEARWATER | FL | USA

The Short Course in Beer

For information, contact Kunati Inc., Book Publishers in Canada.
USA: 13575 58th Street North, Suite 200, Clearwater, FL 33760-3721 USA
Canada: 75 First Street, Suite 128, Orangeville, ON L9W 5B6 CANADA.
E-mail: info@kunati.com.

F I R S T   E D I T I O N

Designed by Kam Wai Yu
Persona Corp. | www.personaco.com

ISBN 978-1-60164-191-5   EAN 9781601641915
Non-Fiction/ Food/Beverages

Published by Kunati Inc. (USA) and Kunati Inc. (Canada).
Provocative. Bold. Controversial.™

http://www.kunati.com

Library of Congress Cataloging-in-Publication Data

Hoffman, L. F. (Lynn F.)
The short course in beer / Lynn Hoffman. -- 1st ed.
    p. cm.
Summary: "A comprehensive guide to the enjoyment and understanding of beer
and beer making around the world, with information about how to taste it,
how it is made, where to find the best and what food to serve with
it"--Provided by publisher.
Includes index.
ISBN 978-1-60164-191-5
1. Beer. I. Title.
TP570.H64 2009
641.6'23--dc22
                              2009012340

To Spencer Hoffman

who has the virtues of

both the malt and the hops

Acknowledgements

Beer Heroes: Dogfish Head Craft Brewed Ales, Victory Brewing, Bella Vista Beer Distributors, Monk's Café, Philadelphia Brewing Company, Yards Brewery, Jim Anderson, Fritz Maytag, Jim Koch, Home Sweet Homebrew, South Philadelphia Taproom, Anchor Brewing, Allagash, Ommegang, and the entire Belgian nation.

Tasting Partners: Joan Adler, Peter Nyheim, Tom Peters, Philip Seitz and the Cliveden Brewers

Contents

Foreword

Why take a short course in beer?

Because it's time to learn what much of the world already knows: beer is complex, delightful and an interesting companion to good food. There are so many people who have discovered this lately that there's a community of beer lovers developing that's devoted to and knowledgeable about good beer. Perhaps it's a coincidence, but this beer-loving community seems attached to some solid, earthy values that seem suddenly appropriate. Beer has become the drink of the energy-conscious, conservation-oriented, planet-sparing gourmet. You can raise a glass of something delicious and be on the side of the angels.

Because pleasure is a vitamin for the soul, and beer is one of the most available, affordable sources of pleasure in the world. I can, without stretching my budget, afford to drink a portion of one of the best beers in the world every single day. The same amount of money will buy a glass of fairly tolerable wine.

If you haven't been paying attention, you might be surprised by all this: beer used to have a bad reputation in some places and it may have even earned that reputation once upon a time. How seriously could we take a drink associated with

- drunken kegger parties
- lager-crazed soccer fans
- freezing-cold tasteless liquid and
- moronic TV commercials?

For years, beer was trapped in a word-association game with the verb "swill." But things have changed. Some of the most creative minds in the world of taste are brewing delicious beer and others are cooking food to complement it. Historic craft-beer traditions are being revived, and new ones are being created. Brewpubs are brewing their own beer and home brew enthusiasts are following suit. There are craft-beer festivals and beer-tasting parties. For the competitive types, there are even competitions and medals and bragging rights. Most of all, there's a lot of startlingly delicious, beautiful beer available for your pleasure. It's time to get in on the fun.

When you finish this book, you will
- know that beer is a truly complex and wonderful drink, worthy of your attention and a companion for the finest food
- be able to make sense of all those wonderful flavors
- know how beer is brewed and where its flavor comes from
- understand the difference between the beers that are worth your time and digestion and the ones that aren't
- have a few thoughts about the place of alcohol in life
- appreciate the intimate relationship between beer and civilization
- know how to find and enjoy a good brew and have a laugh at the rest
- be able to speak knowledgeably about beer, whenever knowledgeable speech is appropriate

Chapter 1

So Much Depends on Beer

When you finish this chapter, you will have
- an understanding of the connection between beer-making and one of mankind's most important inventions
- a sense of the relationship of drunkness and early concepts of the divine
- a healthy dislike for experiments in Prohibition
- some ideas about beer's future
- the beginning of a sense of connoisseurship about that bubbly stuff with the head on it

Beer is, at its best, a philosophers' drink: it stimulates sensitive souls to ask questions, without arousing the arrogance that might lead them to easy answers.

Although we seem to have forgotten it, beer is worth your attention because it can be delightful, but it's also worth a moment's thought because it's been important in the daily lives of many people and cultures for centuries.

For instance: outside of the wine-growing countries of the Mediterranean, most adults in Europe drank beer all day and every day. Both water and milk were potentially dangerous. Beer and wine were both purified as they were made. So up until the seventeenth century, European people—men, women and children—drank some alcoholic beverage: wine, cider or beer. They woke up with it and they went to bed with it. These drinks didn't contain as much alcohol as modern wines and beers, but everyone—mom, dad, the kids, the priest and the king—consumed alcohol all the time.

Consider that life spans were short and that society was patriarchal. That meant that most of the world's business was run by relatively young men who had a bit of a buzz on. In that light, does European history start to make a bit more sense? Does it help you understand bizarre events like the Crusades or the Hundred Years War? If the crew of folks who surrounded you at the pub last night had been in charge, would things have been any different?

Press the rewind button; more questions. When the first agriculturalists settled down to tend and harvest cereals, were they interested in baking bread or in brewing beer? Did the shift from home brewing to industrial production of beer change the economic rôle of women in European society?

Or try this: Does the prevalence of cheap, industrial beer indicate a decline in taste in Western society? Does it point to the primacy of price in consumer decision-making?

Let's take a look at some of the ways that simple beer connects us to the big questions.

Bread, Grain and the Real Staff of Life

Everyone who looks at human history is eventually impressed by the presence of certain milestone events. These are the inventions, occurrences, conceptions and arrangements that make human life forever different. I'm not talking about the millions of ordinary changes that occur to humankind in the course of a year. Instead, I'm referring to really fundamental changes, things that alter the way we relate to one another and the way we see ourselves and the universe.

Printers and their ilk, for instance, are impressed by Gutenberg's invention of moveable type and see it as world-changing. Similar claims are made for the integrated circuit, Marconi's wireless, universal public education and free libraries. Political scientists, historians and journalists like to point to the events of 1776 and 1789 in Philadelphia. Engineers and economists like to cite the Industrial Revolution; other scholars like the opposable thumb and forefinger or the invention of the Pill.

From the perspective of daily life, the most fundamental, revolutionary change was the shift from food gathering to food production. For most of our history we were, like other animals, food finders. We searched for something to eat and then picked it or killed it. At some point in our history, perhaps relying on observations of the natural life cycle of grain-bearing plants, some humans became food cultivators or farmers. For years, pre-historians have insisted that the turn to farming was led by a desire for bread. It is just as likely that it was prompted by the love of beer.

The evidence suggests that the first food we cultivated was a grain, a grass-like plant that bore edible seeds. The seeds of grasses are wonderfully nutritious, even though they require some work to make them palatable. Each seed contains a tiny proteinaceous plant embryo and the carbohydrates and fats necessary to sustain the embryo until it can produce its own food.

It would have been a simple step from observing the relationship of this year's seeds to next year's plants and seeds to helping that relationship along. This new kind of food cultivation had tremendous advantages. By planting and harvesting, you could predict when food would be available and you knew exactly where to find it. The awful periods of starvation that could result from a scarcity of game were a thing of the past. Not only that, but you could produce a lot more calories from farming a small plot of ground than you could extract by hunting and gathering on it. That meant that families didn't have to disperse in order to insure that at least some of them got food.

In fact, it now made sense for at least some members of a group to remain in one place for large parts of the year. Crops were more productive when they were attended and, of course, early farmers wanted to protect their food supply from being harvested by other animals or other men.

The tendency of early food-planters to stay in one place set in motion the chain of events that led to cities and civilization. (The word "civilization" has at its root a Latin word for "city.")

Grains like wheat and barley aren't edible in their raw state: try chewing on a handful of barley from the local health food store and you'll see the problem immediately. Along with cultivation, other technologies emerged or were refined to make grain into human feed. The first grains were probably cooked by parching on a fire-heated rock, but it's not long after true farming begins that fired-clay techniques first develop into the manufacturing of pottery vessels for storing grain and cooking it in water to make a porridge, and the construction of ovens for baking it into true bread.

But the starch load of grain isn't the only nutrition it has to offer. Grain that's been allowed to sprout creates a family of enzymes that—among other things—break those starches down into fermentable sugars. With the help of airborne, ubiquitous yeast, the porridge maker is already on her way to being a brewer. We'll see in chapter 4 just how easy this process is.

The mechanics of this were unknown until the 19th century, when Louis Pasteur discovered the existence of tiny one-celled plants that were at the heart of the fermentation process:

> (M)any varieties of these cellular plants exist, each giving rise to its own particular fermentation. The principal products of these various fermentations, although resembling each other in their nature, differ in their relative proportions and in the accessory substances that accompany them, a fact which alone is sufficient to account for wide differences in the quality and commercial value of alcoholic beverages.
>
> *The Physiological Theory of Fermentation* 1876, Louis Pasteur,

---

All this brewing and baking permitted and encouraged other crafts. Farmers are more efficient than hunters. They produce a lot more food than they consume, so some of their fellow citizens were freed from food making to do other things. The person with a flair for making pots became a full-time potter. The strong but inexpert farmer found employment as a watchman who guarded the fields. Surplus food permitted and encouraged religious and political organization as farmers prayed for good crops and organized armies to defend them. Priests, and then kings appear. Children who were not physically able to hunt could be supported rather than abandoned, and so intellectual and artistic roles became available to play just as there were people to play them.

Civilization requires taxes and records, which in turn led to writing and mathematics and of course to scribes, poets and accountants. The earliest written records are documents involving grain transactions, and these are followed quickly by hymns and recipes.

This big change in human life brought some problems with it. Farming is an early instance of betting everything on a single game. A society that depends on the usually reliable grain crop could be destroyed and dispersed by a single year's crop failure: a peasant farmer is never truly far from starvation. Furthermore, grain, while nutritious, is not a complete food. Meat proteins have all the amino acids that we humans need: grain lacks some of them. The observation that mankind does not live by bread alone is literally as well as spiritually true.

In order to complete the transition to farming, three more problems had to be addressed. Every successful civilization has come up with a solution to all three. The first was the cultivation of a legume, a bean whose protein complemented that in the grain and combined to give humans the protein that they needed. In the Middle East, lentils supplemented wheat and barley; in Asia rice was complemented by millet. In the New World, beans were trained to grow up the stalks of maize (corn).

The second problem was how to keep these stay-at-home farmers from fouling their water supply with waste products. Human and animal waste finds its way into the ground water and contaminates wells. A single sick person can infect everybody by infecting their water with pathogens from feces and urine, and people crowded together are more vulnerable to epidemics than widely scattered hunting bands.

The third part of this grand transition was the abandonment of hunting. Contrary to popular thinking, early man got only a small proportion of his total diet from hunting (most of it came from gathering plants and scavenging the kills of other, more formidable hunters). Hunting and farming are not entirely compatible activities, and the increasingly complex social organization of farmers made the runaway nature of hunting less desirable: you can't have folks going off hunting at critical times in the crop cycle.

But the animal protein that hunting provided was especially well suited to our needs, and the experience of organizing groups to carry out the hunt was and remains intrinsically satisfying. Some people even think that the language skills, social organization and tool manipulation of the hunt are perfect little encapsulations of the skills that first made us human.

The brewing of beer accelerated the last two changes: making the water safe to drink and making home seem sweet indeed. The preparation of beer starts with soaking grain in water at sanitizing temperatures; the beer supply can be safe even when the water it's made from is not. Furthermore the pleasant intoxication and elation that beer provided may have been more of an incentive to settle down than the dull steadiness of bread. It should be no surprise that ex-hunters like a beer or two. For a more sophisticated version of this story, see the article by Sol Katz and Mary Voight at **http://www.shortcourseinbeer.com/ch1**

We are still piecing together the story of our conversion from hunting to agriculture. The archaeologists bring in new pieces from the past all the time. Beer stone, for instance, is a folksy name for calcium oxalate, a precipitate found in the bottom of beer-fermenting and storage vessels. It was the presence of beer stone that enabled Patrick McGovern of the University of Pennsylvania to identify a Mesopotamian pottery fragment from some six thousand years ago as coming from a beer jug.

The early notion that we settled down for bread alone was encouraged by Victorians, who were notoriously uncomfortable with their own jollity. They were also unaware of the nature of the chemical residue or beer stone left in beer pots.

Knowing that porridge and beer are markers of the beginning of civilization, the story of Jacob and Esau takes on a new meaning.

The biblical patriarch Isaac, you'll remember, had two sons, Esau, a hunter, and Jacob, a cook. In the story, Esau sells his birthright for a bowl of Jacob's soup and Jacob then deceives his aged father into giving him his blessing instead of the older Esau. As a pure narrative, the soup itself is a wet-cooked meal, a union of grain and meat, mashed together and maybe even fermented, but there are two more readings of this story.

In the first, the hunter comes home empty-handed and hungry and so surrenders his role as the leader of his tribe in return for a regular meal. In the language of myth, this is a story about the antagonism of hunting and farming and the inevitable succession of one by the other. The second element is the depiction of the guileful farmer/cook and the brutishly stupid hunter.

There is a sense of progress in the story, of a more primitive world order joining with and then giving way to a more advanced one. There is also a profound sense of something lost, of purity and the good old days. The same ambiguity shows up in the Cain and Abel story. The wicked farmer kills the virtuous herdsman but is protected from being punished for his crime.

The Ancients were so taken with the wonder of the changed consciousness that comes from drinking that they endowed wine and beer with gods. The Greeks called the wine god Dionysus (his Roman name was Bacchus).

There is nothing remarkable in this: many ancient peoples saw spirits and gods everywhere. What is astonishing is the character of the gods of alcoholic drink. Let's take the Greeks as an example since we know them best.

Most of the Greek gods are remote from human affairs, showing up like bill collectors to remind their devotees of missed sacrifices or dilapidated temples. The reminders were often in the form of disease, famine or other catastrophe. For the Greeks, a good god was one who kept his distance. The gods had no moral message and they certainly inspired no emotion in their worshippers other than anxiety. Dionysus, on the other hand, is a very personal god. He calls himself the Happy One. He speaks of balance, sounding for all the world like a college professor busily professing moderation. His worship is a party, not a sacrifice. He enters the body of his worshippers with the wine and he lifts their spirits.

There is a curious parallel to explore here. Dionysus is the son of a mortal woman and a god. He dies a terrible death: he was torn to pieces repeatedly and always resurrected. At his festival, jars of water are miraculously turned into wine. Most importantly, Dionysians feel the presence of the god inside them.

As you can imagine, there's a lot of controversy about what the parallels between the life stories of Dionysus and Jesus mean. Was Christianity derived from the religion of the drunken god? Did they both partake in ideas that were current at the time?

In Julius Caesar's time, Dionysus came to be known as Bacchus and he had become a savior whose worship guaranteed a life after death. (Compare that with the apparently more frivolous and much more recent story of John Barleycorn in appendix B, whose body is transformed into human food and drink.) His rites included a communion meal at which the god's flesh was eaten and his blood drunk in the form of wine. As the cult of the classical gods declined in

Rome, the worship of Bacchus increased, only to go underground when the competing Christian religion was made official in the fourth century.

Against the grim reality that was the common person's life in ancient Rome, alcohol must have thrown a particularly appealing and diverting light. Even in happy circumstances, alcohol lightens the spirits, soothes anxieties and lubricates the social instincts. It makes the shy person outgoing, the sad person jolly and the dull person witty.

This effect, and beer's fortunate talent as a partner to food and feasting, make it a very social beverage. It is this ability of alcohol to demolish inhibitions, inspire enthusiasm and encourage sociability that lies at the heart of the beverage business. People drink in company because both the drink and the company become more pleasant in the process. It's hard to avoid quoting A.E. Housman, and in fact most beer authors do:

And malt does more than Milton can
To justify God's ways to man.

Most beer lovers neglect the next lines, which have a gloomier take on beer's contribution:

Ale, man, ale's the stuff to drink
For fellows whom it hurts to think:
Look into the pewter pot
To see the world as the world's not.
—Terence, This is Stupid Stuff (1896)

But the more poetic defense is by the Roman, Orazio. Known in the English-speaking world as Horace, he tells us that alcohol:

unlocks secrets,

bids hopes be fulfilled,
thrusts the coward onto the battle-field,
takes the load from anxious hearts.
Who have flowing cups not made eloquent?
Whom has it not made free from the most grinding,
pinching poverty?
Epistles, V

Housman (who, incidentally, translated Horace) had reason
enough to be gloomy, but Horace's life took some ugly turns too.
We'll talk more about this complicated business in chapter 3.

Local Brewers

In the thirteenth century English village of Elton, one craft was
more widely practiced than all the rest together. Every village had
its brewers. Elton, a village of some six hundred people, had its own
kiln for drying malt and almost all of the brewers were women.

Beer was as important as bread to the villagers, but where mill-
ing and bread baking were sternly guarded monopolies of the lord,
brewing was barely regulated and not taxed, except in the indirect
form of fines for giving short measure.

The practice was to brew a batch of ale, hang a sign and be open
for business as long as the ale lasted. When the sign was out, the ale-
tasters arrived. Ale-taster was the only office in the medieval village
that was open to women, and every village had its ale-tasters.

In 1279, the ale-tasters of Elton indicted twenty-three people, all
of them women, for brewing offenses. The Manor Record shows
"Allota is a common brewer at a penny and sometimes at a halfpen-
ny, and sold before the tasting and sometimes made (the ale) weak.
Therefore she is fined two shillings."

The alewife or brewster seems to have represented an island of
individual initiative. She would have to have been a pretty tough
customer herself; Elton's magisterial records are full of after-drink

quarrels, misdemeanors and injuries.

The alewife remained a stock figure in folklore until the industrial revolution. In Elizabethan England, beer making was still a housewife's task, although a great house might employ a visiting brewer.

The notorious "alewives of Fleet Street" were probably not brewers but hawkers of ale. By the fifteenth century, only fifteen of London's 300 brewers were women. With industrialization, beer became big business and the men were soon in charge.

Beer and its Enemies

Like other milestone inventions (fire, automobiles and the iPod for instance), alcohol is not entirely a blessing. Right next to the lightened spirits and occasional hilarity of moderate drinking lie the recklessness of excessive drinking and the tragedy of habitual drunkenness.

Even alcohol's manifest virtues are denied by some. Many people find the altered state of consciousness that alcohol produces to be threatening. It brings out things in themselves and other people that they would rather not have called forth. People consuming alcohol are more likely to be sexual and boisterous. They're also more likely to be aggressive or otherwise obnoxious. If you've never met an inhibition you didn't like, then the moderately disinhibiting effect of alcohol is going to be very scary.

It's a short step from being repelled by one's own impulses to wishing to eradicate or at least camouflage them in others. In the United States, that impulse, coupled with a racist prejudice against wine-drinking Italians and Jews and beer-drinking Irish and Germans, led to the Volstead Act in 1919. This law made the sale and possession of alcoholic beverages illegal in the United States. It ushered in an era called Prohibition

Prohibition was a thirteen-year period in which there was no legal beer, wine (apart from that used sacramentally) or spirits consumed in the United States. It had profound and lasting effects on the American beverage industry, and its underlying prejudice is still alive and well. Here are some of the ways that Prohibition affected the industry and the nation.

- It created an enormously profitable illegal business. The profits from that business funded the establishment and later expansion of organized crime. You might say that the Volstead Act funded the Mafia.
- It destroyed two already established industries. Wineries and breweries folded, vineyards were dug up and converted to table grapes (or thick skinned wine varieties that could be shipped east by rail for the use of home winemakers). It similarly destroyed many local breweries that were not rich enough to invent a new business to tide them through the dry years. Winemakers and brewers left the industry and turned their talents to other ends. When Prohibition ended there was a depression going on, and most of the breweries and wineries were never re-established. In 1910, there were 1,570 breweries in the US. In 1934, a year after repeal, only 714 survived. In St. Louis, twenty breweries dwindled to eight by the end of 1933.

  The pattern was repeated across the country; local brews were replaced by national brands whose strength was their advertising, not their flavor. Instead of lots of regional beers brewed to delight a small audience, we ended up with a few national brands designed to avoid offending a large one.
- It changed American tastes and made us a nation of whiskey drinkers. Since it's easier to traffic in small volumes of a highly concentrated illegal substance, distilled spirits became more available and more desired.
- It defined a legitimate and venerable pleasure as illegal and immoral. Fermented fruit became forbidden fruit. This intrusion of morality into what was formerly the matter-of-fact persists to this day. Recently, a proposed new Federal tax on wine was

widely discussed as a "sin tax."

We learned our national lesson so well in the 20s that we repeated it in the 80s. This time we cracked down on bulky marijuana and so made it very profitable to import the compact cocaine. A mildly intoxicating homegrown substance was replaced with a highly addictive one, and incidentally, we replaced the threat posed by hippies in tie-dyed tee shirts with that of Colombian drug lords commanding their own private armies.

> On 5 December, 1933, Prohibition officially ended. H.L. Mencken, the Sage of Baltimore, celebrated Repeal by drinking a glass of water. "My first," he said, "in thirteen years."

The Future

At beer tastings and festivals these days, there's a tremendous sense of optimism among beer lovers. Not only is there more good beer around than ever before, but the evidence of the senses and the statistics is that there's more to come. Consider:

- Beer consumption is decreasing, but the consumption of beer with flavor is increasing. Americans are drinking less per capita and less overall but more of what we drink is good beer.
- There's an incredible sense of newness and growth in the air. New brewpubs are opening at the rate of more than one a week.* On a list of the top 168 breweries in the country, twenty-nine were not in existence a year ago.
- The American thirst for good beer has sparked a new flow of imports. Small breweries in Belgium, England and Germany are sending part of their production, and we are drinking it fast enough to insure that bottles contain fresh and drinkable beer.
- There have been confirmed sightings of beer snobs. There is a certain pleasure in connoisseurship, in studying and knowing a thing well enough to get as much pleasure from your knowl-

edge of it as you do from the thing itself. There's also a bit of cultural and political statement involved. In an age when mass pleasures like television are becoming more feeble and homogeneous, the very act of discrimination becomes a form of protest. At a time when mass marketing of food produces a product so disgusting that it has to be wrapped in distracting gimmicks to be sold, the mere fact of paying attention to what you eat and drink and telling the truth about taste is a revolutionary act.

Quite apart from tickling the brain, becoming knowledgeable about something as joyfully frivolous as beer gives us a chance to be one up on those less learned. From One Up, it's a short trip to Better Than, and pretty soon you've picked up that piece of Excess Baggage called a Sense of Superiority.

Of course the more that a thing is discussed, the more common its knowledge becomes and the less exclusive is the club of those in the know. This means that there's a constant pressure for new things to be hip about, for new arenas in which to display your sophistication. It's too late to reserve one of the first seats on the beer connoisseur bandwagon, (See all those people in flannel shirts harumphing over the dark brown stuff in their glasses?) but there are a few choice slots left in the specialty section.

Speculations about the future tend to be optimistic extensions of the present: There's a brewpub in every neighborhood, a microbrewery in every small town. You can touch the screen on your phone and order a six-pack of any beer in the world. Your local brewery will make up a special batch for you and your friends. Even the supermarket shelves will be stocked with interesting beer. The dominance of the giant breweries will have either faded like shadows retreating from the sunrise or continue and be based on variety rather than uniformity of product. Or maybe not.

A lot of the people who are looking to this millennium are veterans of the sixties. They should know better. There are some built-in limits to how far the beer revolution can proceed. The most important limit lies in the incredible dominance of the market by the biggest producers.

The Big Three control almost 92 percent of the domestic beer market. Marketing giants like Anheuser-Busch may lose their independence, but they are unlikely to die in their sleep. As the market shrinks and the competition increases, they are bound to notice and respond.

What will that response be? These are giant organizations, so you can expect the response to be glacial. They got where they are by making one kind of product and they are likely to see their own future in terms of that same product. When craft beers accounted for 1 percent of the market and imports for another 4 percent, a beer executive in Milwaukee was able to scoff at the size of the competition and proclaim no interest in producing better beer.

Look for some timid moves, like the introduction of mock premiums and lobbying for higher taxes on microbreweries. Look for brewers to try to expand their traditional beer-drinking base by going after wine drinkers and women. Look for advertising campaigns that try to link the Big Three brands with Truth, Justice and the American Way.

When mere advertising proves to be just a palliative, there will probably be some structural moves to address the problem. I'll be watching for big brewers to buy up little ones on very generous terms. Some small brewers will become very rich takeover targets. I think it's possible that a few wineries will get caught in the fever. Could a brewer resist acquiring the upscale marketing expertise of wine makers like Tim Mondavi, Randall Graham or Joseph Phelps?

Ultimately, the challenge of small breweries to large ones will be met by shakeups in the way brewing business is done. We may see the big three spin off their own microbreweries. We will certainly see a flurry of new product launches. I would expect to see rich, malty stouts and Belgian ales designed to appeal to the older, more sophisticated consumer who isn't drinking much beer now. Some brewers may try to exploit ethnic and regional differences in tastes. For instance, someone is sure to develop distinctive beers for the Spanish-speaking Caribbean/South Florida Markets. Licensing agreements with foreign brands are possible too. A brand from Jamaica, Korea or Kenya could be brewed in the US (remember, a beer is just a recipe; see chapter 4) to appeal to a particular constituency without the problems of importing.

Finally, I think homebrewing and related very small-scale brewing operations are going to occupy a tiny but secure niche in the beer market.

Golden Age of Beer

The good news is that the good old days are probably now. While it's true that there's a lot of heavily advertised bad beer and a lot of malt liquor that's nothing more than a drug with bubbles, it's also true that there's a startling number of very good beers. The best news is that transportation and communication have made the good beers a lot more available than they ever were.

The caring consumer has sources of information to help her take advantage of the new opportunities. There are some three dozen Beerfests held annually in various parts of the country. Want to know more about them? Consult a *brewspaper*. (You can find some listed in the resources section at the back of this book.) There are hundreds of taverns that cater to the beer lover and scores of beer distributors. Some of the taverns, called brewpubs, brew the beer they sell. Others stress the artisanal, hand-crafted products of microbreweries.

There's an association of homebrewers that hosts a network of brew clubs. They have their own magazine, called *Zymurgy*, and are served by a growing number of knowledgeable homebrew supply stores. (One of these stores, Home Sweet Homebrew, has been in business in Philadelphia since 1986.) There are sponsored homebrew competitions to improve the breed. You can become acquaint-

Protecting the grain from the mice.

ed with new styles of beer and have your own brewing critiqued and improved. You may find out that homebrewed beer is often better than anything available commercially and usually at least as good.

Your chances of getting a really superb glass of beer, brewed, handled and served with care, are greater than they have been for decades. Your chance of having a choice of outstanding examples of various beer styles is greater than it's ever been. All signs are that the situation is only going to get better. A book like the one you're holding in your hands would have been unthinkable just a few years ago.

There are things that you can do to make a good situation better. One that comes immediately to mind is demanding that brewers supply information about ingredients and date of bottling. (See Just Say Know, below.) Another is to learn more about what makes great beer great and ask for better beer wherever you buy beer—the supermarket, the liquor store or the tavern.

Hogarth's engraving of the mythical Beer Street, characterized by ale, prosperity and family values.

Macho Man and the Alewives

Beer is remarkable too for the gender and social class stereotypes that it calls into question. Beer is the only product I know of whose light, flavorless and effeminate versions are downed by "real men" and whose hearty, eccentric, flavorful, individualistic and big-bodied manifestations are favored by nerds in suspenders. Go figure.

My secret suspicion is that this is the beginning sign of a major change. One day, the paradigm is going to shift and Lexus-loads full of young MBAs are going to be driving through working class neighborhoods, waving their bottles of Golden Monkey, Boon Faro and ESA and shouting insults at the working folks drinking industrial beers on the stoop. ("Nyahhh! you drink like a girl!! Where did you learn to drink beer? The union hall?") Stay tuned.

Small Beer

By the seventeenth century, it was common practice to refer to "strong beer," "table beer," "ship's beer" and "small beer." The distinctions were based on the amount of sugar per volume of brewing liquid and therefore, on the strength of the resulting beer. Small beer was the lightest, least flavorful, least alcoholic beer and the one with the shortest shelf life. Until the seventeenth century, small beer was the universal beverage of the Northern European world, serving every man, woman and child where sodas, coffee and juices serve us now. To say that something was small beer was to say that it was an ordinary matter, not remarkable and of no great concern.

Shakespeare liked the expression. He has Iago dismiss fair and virtuous women as fit to "suckle fools and chronicle small beer." The last is a reference to over-meticulous keeping of household accounts. In the famous scene from Henry VI Part 2 where Dick the Butcher proposes killing all the lawyers, Jack Cade promises that when he is crowned king "I will make it a felony to drink small beer." Even worse than the penalty for felony is this epitaph from a graveyard in Winchester.

Here sleeps in peace a Hampshire Grenadier,
Who caught his death by drinking cold small beer
Soldiers, take heed from his untimely fall
And when you're hot, drink strong or not at all.

What do Women Drink?

Until recently, the answer has been "anything but beer." In focus groups and marketing surveys, women say they don't drink beer because they don't like the taste.

This raises an interesting question that goes right to the heart of the nature/nurture question. When you give a beer tasting, the crowd is at least as single sexed as the one at the Outdoor Show. Even allowing for the fact that men drink more drinks with alcohol than women, how come almost everybody who likes beer is a man? Do men and women simply have different taste buds?

One possible answer has to do with adolescent drinking rites. Hardly anybody who didn't sip it as a child likes their first taste of beer. Beer's bitterness is something most of us have to learn to appreciate. Teenaged boys learn to stifle their initial disgust with beer much as they learn to shake off that hurt finger, put the glove back on and go back to their position. The payoff is in being part of the crowd, feeling more grown up and manly and of course, the pleasant buzz of disinhibiting intoxication.

Teenaged girls taste beer and for the most part say something like "yuck." They may endure other discomforts for other ends, but swallowing yucky stuff isn't on their list, at least not initially. They may learn to tolerate beer as the drink of low-budget sociability, but little girls don't romanticize their hardships in the same way little boys do. No young woman makes it to graduate school dreaming of an endless stream of Old Milwaukee.

Women's reluctance to drink beer has changed the industry by focusing its marketing efforts. Some would say the focus is on men; others might claim that the focus is on the adolescent boy preserved inside each man.

By the way, in case you think that there's some natural gender preference involved here, remember that in the first Elizabethan Age, beer seems to have suited women very well. The queen's maids of honour were allotted a daily ration: two gallons of a beer called Doble-Doble.

Who Buys Beer?

Men buy beer. According to the Beer Institute, in supermarkets, where men spend 28.7 percent of the total dollar volume, they spend 54.7 percent of the beer dollar volume. An often-quoted statistic has women accounting for only 25 percent of beer consumption in the US.

There is some change in the air. Some new products seem to be gaining acceptance among female drinkers. The estimable beer writer Lew Bryson has suggested that women will pay more attention to beer as soon as beer starts paying more attention to them with marketing campaigns that address women's concerns. Since women control more than half the personal wealth in this country, it seems likely that brewers will increasingly look for the answer to the question: What do women drink?

Wine and Beer

It's hard not to compare these two, as if they were first cousins whose family resemblance was much less interesting than their quirky differences. This may be because we can sense magnetic poles of difference in the feelings attached to these drinks.

In places where there were choices, wine was for the rich folks. This is not a recent development. Athenaeus, writing some 1700 years ago, observed of the ancient Egyptians that

A way was found among them to help those who could not afford

wine, namely, to drink that wine made from barley.
Sophists at Dinner, Book I

In European countries where wine was not made, rich people imported it, and even bad wine always cost more than beer. In wine-growing countries, no one imported beer.

In places like Germany, where both were available, wine was the cultural expression of the turn to Rome, beer an expression of the turn to the pagan north.

In vine-worthy France, the Romans founded a settlement that they called a province, a part of their own world. We call it Provence. In the inhospitable north, they called their towns colonies. We memorialize the difference in place names like Cologne. Pliny, that most roman of Romans, spoke of beer in the same way we might speak of a hallucinogenic vine cultivated by mud-daubed blowgun hunters.

The nations of the West also have their own intoxicant, made from grain soaked in water. There are a number of ways of making it in the various provinces of Gaul and Spain ... Egypt also has devised for itself similar drinks made from grain.
Natural History: Book XIV

The English, or at least the spokesmen for the commoner sort, have cherished a xenophobic dislike of wine.

Thy wanton grapes we do detest:
Here's richer juice from Barley press'd
Anonymous Poet, quoted in *The Curiosities of Ale and Beer* by John Bickerdyke 1889

Beer and wine still represent some uncrossable cultural and symbolic gulfs. In America the two drinks have pretty well defined contexts and most of us know where the two belong without giving the matter much thought.

Beer advertising has done its share to make sure that beer stays on the lower end of the taste/style/class continuum. Here's an example involving the association of a product with the rear end of a flatulent horse.

http://www.youtube.com/watch?v=EUtwNtE1NBA&feature=related

You might wonder who watches this and decides it would be fun to taste the featured product.

Then there's the matter of food and drug administration. Wine goes with food; most of it is consumed with meals. Beer is apart from it, drunk by itself or with salty snacks. Marketers know this by heart. Ads for wine show the dinner table; ads for beer show the great outdoors or the tavern.

There have been attempts to sell beer for dinner and wine for cooling off after a hot day at the beach. They haven't worked because fundamentally, these two wonderful drinks are built differently to serve very different purposes. This situation will change only when beer itself changes.

One astonishing aspect of the beer/wine dichotomy is that the people who are supporting the good beer movement in this country seem to be drawn from wine families as much as beer families. Some beers, selling at $8 a bottle in bars, are hardly drinks for the working man (in fact part of their appeal may be in their high price). A similar volume of well-made wine can be found in wine shops for as little as $2.

Parody

Many beer lovers think that beer ads are notoriously silly. As the media involved become more electronic, the ads become sillier still. There are a lot of reasons for this, but at the heart of the issue are two facts. The first is that men drink beer to enjoy the taste and/or to enjoy a mild intoxication in the company of their friends. The second is that unfortunately most beers don't taste very good, and calling attention to their flavor is probably not a good way to sell them.

You can't make too much of the "just us guys" theme either: we are still nervous about the erotic implications of a bunch of men removing themselves from the world of women and slamming down a six-pack or two in the woods.

So beer ads (in America of recent years, at least) have been forced to skirt the real issues like taste and talk about men's fantasies. The crowds of attractive young women prancing around with beer bottle labels visible don't look like any beer bar crowd I've ever seen. Those fellows whose seaplane is parked in the cool Canadian lake are more likely to be drinking '89 Haut-Brion or Anchor Steam than the discount priced beer in the ad. And so on.

All of this, if you will take it as true, obliges us to look at two more questions. First, if the ads are all that shallow, how come they sell beer? This may not be a question at all. It may be its own answer. Inanity in beer ads may be an asset, not a problem. See Who Buys Beer?

The second and far more important question is this: How come there are no parodies of beer ads? With all the comic talent running around loose in this great land of ours, where are the spoofs, the parodies and the send-ups?

How come I can watch Saturday Night TV and never see the garbage delivery man who knocks on your door and announces "This Crud's for You"? Where on the Comedy Channel is the gentle understanding therapist who approves of your phobia saying "It's the right fear now"?

Conspiracy theories abound. In spite of them, I think the silver, I mean single-bullet answer, is that parody relies on taking silly things even further out on the frontier of ridiculousness. When it comes to beer ads, there may not be any place left to go. What can you do to parody a party that seems to revolve around a lot of pretty women frantically courting the attention of a stupefied bull terrier? Do you have any ideas about spoofing the football game played between two teams of long-necked bottles wearing helmets?

The conceptual problem is highlighted by the fact that one conscious attempt at an ad that was a parody of other ads—the famous Swedish Bikini Team ad—was taken seriously.

And Finally, Urination

Beer makes you piss. There. I said it and I'm glad. There are at least three biological reasons why this is so.

- The volume of liquid involved when you sit down to drink beer is likely to be greater than the volume consumed when you get together with some friends for tea or a nice glass of water.
- One of the ingredients of beer is hops, and hops is a diuretic.
- Alcohol suppresses the levels of the hormone ADH, which is a water-retaining hormone. When you make less ADH, your body gets a signal to dump some of its normal load of water. Incidentally, this is why one of the symptoms reported by overindulgers is a sense of thirst that seems to come from the level of one's very body cells.

Discussion Questions
1. If beer is important, shouldn't it be rich and flavorful?
2. Can you imagine a modern religion with beer drinking at its center?
3. If beer is so central to the rise of civilization, how has it come to seem so uncivilized?
4. Have you ever seen a beer ad that respected your intelligence? What was the beer behind it? How about the stupidest ad that's out right now? Do you remember the brand it advertises?

Chapter 2

The Taste of Beer

When you finish this chapter, you will have
- a routine for tasting beer that will make you look and feel like a connoisseur
- a new awareness of both the sense of taste and the sense of smell
- an appreciation of how these two senses combine to make the experience we call flavor
- the beginning of a vocabulary with which to describe what you're tasting
- a healthy skepticism about food fakelore like the "Tongue Map"
- a good sense of the ingredients that put that flavor in your beer and how they do it

You may not have enjoyed your first glass of beer. Bitterness, which is a fairly recent innovation in beer, is something of an acquired taste. Even after you grew to like other sharp tastes, you may not have enjoyed that first bitter smack of beer.

Learning to drink beer in late twentieth century America meant learning to ignore the unpleasant taste in order to enjoy the benefits of feeling masculine, grown up, one of the gang, and a bit giddy. Many of the people reading this book have had their taste preferences imprinted by relatively tasteless beer, the kind that's inexpensive to make and has to be served very cold. Naturally, the people who sell you beer say very little about taste and a great deal about the joys of feeling masculine, grown up and one of the gang. They prefer, for a variety of reasons, not to talk directly about feeling giddy, but instead to imply it by the slightly hilarious behavior of the models in the commercials. The drink that was once the lure that brought us to agriculture and civilization had become the tasteless source of a cheap intoxicated buzz.

One unfortunate consequence of all this is that when you grow up, calm down and start paying attention to flavor, there's not much beer out there that tastes very good. If you decide you want beer with flavor, you'll have to go looking for it.

Finding it isn't easy. In many parts of the country and in a lot of saloons anywhere, there's no beer with flavor to be had. Sometimes asking for, or admitting to a preference for flavor with your beer can be socially awkward. You have just become a member of a minority group. If it's your first time being part of one, you may find it odd.

Fortunately, as with membership in other minorities, there are payoffs. There is a certain clubbiness to places where the better beers are found. There's a camaraderie among those who, as amateurs or professionals, brew the better stuff. There's the exhilarating feeling of being in the aesthetic vanguard and having the chance to buy books like this one.

And of course, the beer is better.

Tasting and Drinking

If you think of beer in terms of a noisy fraternity basement or a paper cup at the ball game, the idea of a beer tasting may seem a little strange. Beer is something you drink: who tastes it? Until a few decades ago, that was a fair observation. Beer was the drink of sociability: it was far more important that we were all drinking together than that the beer tasted of anything in particular. In fact, the old-fashioned ideal of ice-cold beer was both a tribute to and insurance of a drink that didn't taste like anything in particular. But times have changed. Beer is for pleasure now, and a great deal of the pleasure is in the tasting.

Wine tasters, who already know what all the fun is about, are in for a special surprise when they start to pay attention to beer. Wine varies from year to year depending on the quality of the raw material, which differs which each year's weather. What you learned last year about Château Shazam doesn't mean much when it comes to this year's vintage. Brewers, on the other hand, make a fetish of consistency. Even the meanest, most insipid industrial plonk is presided over by a team of brewing scientists who make sure that every batch tastes just as vacant as the last.

> "It takes a good brewer to make good beer. The weird thing is that it also takes a good brewer to make bad beer."
> —Manny Cardoso

Barring sudden shortages of key ingredients, you can be sure that your favorite beer will usually taste the way you remember it and that any variations in flavor will probably have to do with a loss of freshness or bad storage and serving practices or changes mandated by the marketing department. (See chapter 5: Enjoying Beer)

The Taste is in the Ingredients

The taste of beer comes—not surprisingly—from its ingredients. The three flavorful ingredients of most beer are malt, hops and yeast. Some beers use grains other than malt and some beers use seasonings other than hops. Yeast can be nothing more than a workman-like little alcohol producer, or it can be a master chef.

Malt contributes aromas and flavors that remind you of breakfast cereal, bread, caramel or toasted and roasted bread (In fact, some of the flavor of cereal, caramel and bread comes from extracts of malted grain). Beer's mouth feel—its thickness or body—also comes from malt.

Hops: bitterness is hops' traditional contribution to flavor, but citrus, herbal, grass-clippings and floral aromas can be derived from different hop varieties.

Yeast: a commercial yeast guide from Wyeast Laboratories, a

supplier to home- and craft-brewers, lists yeasts that create citrus, vanilla, sulfur, fruit, butter, nut, butterscotch, banana, bubblegum, lactic acid and even malt flavors produced by their products. A very few beers are fermented with bacteria as well as yeast and you might notice sour or musty aromas.

Most brewers try for a balance of all three components, but some beers emphasize one factor or the other. If you'd like to taste these characteristics in exaggerated form, you might try the following styles (for more about beer styles, see Chapter 7)

Malt: In fact, any high-alcohol beer is likely to have a strong malt character, but it's more likely to stand out in these styles: Scotch Ales, Belgian Abbey Doubles, German Bocks, Porters and Imperial Stouts.

Hops bitterness: India Pale Ale, Irish Dry Stout

Hops aroma: Pilsner

Hops bitterness and aroma: American Pale Ale, ordinary English Bitter.

Yeast: The spicy flavors of Farmhouse Ales and the rich taste of Trappists come from their special yeasts. Cloudy Hefeweizens and some other wheat beers get their intense aromatics from yeast.

What is Taste?

The act we call tasting is really an assembly of sensory impressions. Taste itself occurs on the tongue. There are specific receptors for bitterness, sweetness, acidity, saltiness and the pungent savoriness of umami. Apart from those five, most of the experience of taste comes from aromas, and a distinct component comes from the sensations of touch: temperature, astringency, thickness (body) and the prickliness of carbonation.

The Tongue Map and Other Fakelore.

You may have seen a drawing of the tongue with different areas assigned to different taste sensations. Sweetness is on the front tip, bitterness along the sides in the back and so on. It's an interesting thought, it sounds like it could be useful, but it's dead wrong. In general, we taste most tastes everywhere on the tongue. The story of how this particular weird idea has been passed down and accepted uncritically is a good cautionary tale. In fact, there are enough stories like The Tongue Map that they have their own category: they're called fakelore. Beware of folks who want to sound smart by passing along the bull: watch out for the Tongue Mappers!

(Oh, and try to be aware when you're being one yourself.)

The sad fact is that we don't actually taste most of what we eat and drink. Our attention is chronically elsewhere and we often eat and drink without awareness. This in itself is not necessarily bad: a lot of what's out there to eat wouldn't stand much attention. If you don't believe me, buy a fast food hamburger and eat it slowly, relishing the taste and describing the individual flavors. Chances are that you won't make it to the second bite, or that you'll quickly find distractions.

Our inattention has other roots too; we are a busy people and a self-conscious one to boot. Our minds are often involved in things far away from the here and now: it's as if we lived most of our lives in a fog of words running through our minds and never actually experienced the world around us.

One of the wonders of beer is that it invites us to stop, slow down and pay attention. If we accept the invitation, the reward is not only the beer itself, but a moment of being fully present in the world.

So to get to this genuine tasting we actually may have to learn how to taste. A good place to start is to look at the strategies we develop to avoid tasting. Maybe you remember having to swallow a bad-tasting medicine. If you did, you probably learned to chill the medicine first so you didn't smell the awful stuff. Maybe you held your nose and bolted the stuff down in a hurry so the taste didn't have time to make you gag. You might have immediately followed the dose with a treat like ice cream or a cookie that overrode the bad taste.

To get the most out of the taste of beer, you can do just the opposite. You allow yourself all the time in the world; you focus your attention and eliminate distractions. Hold the beer in your mouth for a few extra heartbeats, and let yourself be delighted if delight is in order. You might want to avoid distractions too: skip the perfume and the after-shave and turn down the music. Think of the ideal environment—a shady spot at the edge of the woods on a warm afternoon, for instance—and bring yours in line with it.

The most important thing is that to get the full experience of the beer, you have to hold off on deciding whether you like it or not. Turn the rush to judgment into a slow, deliberate, even reluctant march. The minute you decide that you "like" the beer (or not) you stop noticing the beer and start paying attention to how clever you are, how absolutely right on. We all tend to fall in love with our own ideas, and ideas are the enemy of perception.

To taste your beer, you'll probably want to pour it into a glass first. It would be a shame to waste all that yummy aroma by drinking from the bottle.

The Color of Beer

Look at the beer in your glass. The colors that you see are partly a by-product of the flavors that the brewer wanted to put in the beer. Darkly toasted grains contribute deep brown color as well as flavor. They may also be a part of the brewer's design for the beer, a signal to you about what to expect. Remember that color is a hint, not a sure-fire indication of flavor, sweetness or alcohol content.

Color is a Liar

One of the darkest commercial beers in the world is Guinness Stout. Contrary to what you might think, it's a moderately bitter, bone-dry, low-alcohol, low-calorie brew. There's a beer from Belgium called Duvel (DOO-vl) that's pale as death, thick in the mouth, slightly sweet and irresistible. One commercial brewer in the US bought out an Irish brand name. They brewed a product here under that name that was pretty much the same as their regular beer but with a slightly reddish color. Many people preferred it to the brewery's other offering, but tasted in opaque glasses most folks couldn't tell the difference. Eyes don't have taste buds.

Whatever the color, the beer may be crystal clear or have various degrees of opalescence. (Those ain't clouds, they're opals.) A beer that's perfectly clear will have been filtered to make it so: you may wonder if anything else was taken out in the process. A little fog in your glass may suggest that the beer has a distinct body or thickness in the mouth.

All beer that's filtered is cold-filtered. Any advertising that suggests that cold-filtering of beer is something special might as well boast of the beer's being wet or having bubbles.

Beer's Bouquet

If you're not tasting from a full glass, swirl the beer to increase evaporation and release the bouquet. You can only smell what's in the air. This is a good time to mention that if your beer is too cold, you won't be able to smell much. (See Serving Temperature in chapter 5)

Taste the Foam

The head of foam at the top of a glass of beer is the romantic signature of the drink itself. We drink lots of things with bubbles, but only beer separates a foamy layer from the rest of the drink and offers itself up for tasting. The bittering acids that give beer its tangy, mouth-watering quality will be more concentrated in the head of foam. Taste it first and savor the sharpness suspended in air. It's quite a remarkable sensation, both dilute in moisture and concentrated in flavor.

> Some wine lovers make a distinction between the aroma of a grape and the bouquet of the finished wine. In beerland, the words are synonyms.

Sniffing Beer

You'll need a certain kind of glass to get this sniffing business right. Since a cool temperature is part of the experience of beer, the aroma that comes off the cool beer is stingy. There's a particular

A selection of proprietary glassware. Courtesy of Bella Vista Beer Distributors.

kind of glass that makes it a little more generous. Several of these glasses are pictured on previous page. What most of them have in common is a tulip shape that helps concentrate the aroma as it rises from the beer. Put your nose over the beer and take a mighty sniff. If your beer is at the right serving temperature, you should notice several appetizing aromas. Loud, greedy snorts that would be inappropriate at the dinner table are just fine at a beer tasting. You'll notice that if you sniff a second time, your impression is diminished; a third attempt and you notice even less. The sense of smell fatigues quickly. So get what you can while you can. (And try not to extend that aphorism beyond its appropriate reach.)

One exception to the tulip-shaped rule is the chalice-like goblet from Chimay. (See photo chapter 5) Chimay is brewed by members of a Catholic religious order and the shape of the glass may have for them connotations that are powerfully symbolic. As far as I know, no one has complained about the taste of Chimay beers being diminished by the shape of the glass.

The receptors for your sense of smell are located on a small patch of flesh called the olfactory epithelium. It's inside your skull behind your nose and at the same level as your eyes. It's a few centimeters square and it contains some five million receptor cells, about the same number that you'd find in the nose of a mouse. (Mice will drink beer if given a chance; they just don't get to drink mine.) In normal breathing, only 5 to 10 percent of inhaled air reaches this sensory receptor. You can increase the amount of stimulation at the epithelium by a factor of ten simply by using your nose to take sharp, deep sniffs before you drink. Don't decide if you like the aromas: just try to notice and name them.

If you notice aromas but can't quite place them, look at the New Taster's Checklist at the end of this chapter for some hints. For starters, see if the aromas remind you of:

Fruit

Spice

Herbs

Grain

If you notice a fruity aroma, for instance, it doesn't mean that somebody slipped a few Macintoshes in with the malt. It's just evidence of the fact that fermentation creates more than just alcohol and that some common aromas show up again and again in wine and beer.

The Nobel Prize in Medicine in 2004 was awarded to the folks who discovered how the sense of smell actually works. It turns out that the olfactory patch contains approximately 400 different kinds of receptors. Each receptor responds to only one kind of molecule in the air. These receptors pass messages along to parts of the brain. Each brain area, called a glomerulus, receives impulses from only one kind of receptor. All of the 10,000 odors that we recognize are built up from combinations of these receptors and pathways.

What are you smelling? Your nose is being tickled by chemicals. For the full story of how they got in your glass, go to chapter 4: How Beer is Made.

Sipping Beer

If you're just starting to taste beer, this may seem like the best part. Take a generous, mouth-filling sip of beer and move it around in your mouth to get acquainted with it and also to increase your sense of its aroma. Keep the beer moving: just like smell, your sense of taste gets fatigued too. Pay attention to all the flavors without deciding if you "like" the beer or not. Now is the time to notice the physical sensations: how does the beer feel in your mouth? Do you notice a bitter pinch in the back of your mouth? Maybe the beer is so spritzy that it feels like soda pop or perhaps it has only a gentle carbonation? Is the carbonation in proportion to the flavor or does it overwhelm it? Does the beer feel thin and watery or is there some substance to it? We call this sensation the "body." Thin-bodied beers feel like water or skim milk in the mouth; big-bodied beers are more like cream.

With your mouth full of beer, part your lips a little and pull in some air over the beer. (Try not to dribble down your shirt, it could spoil your concentration.) Exhale through your nose. The beer has warmed in your mouth now and its aroma has intensified. You'll be smelling it again as the air brings the aromatic molecules around to your olfactory patch through passages in the nose. Because you experience it with the flavors of the beer alive in your mouth, the "back smell" can be more intense than that tentative first sniff you took a minute before.

This little maneuver—hold beer in mouth, open lips, inhale, close lips, exhale through nose—is worth practicing, both for the pleasure and for avoiding having beer squirt out your nose.

High alcohol beers should have correspondingly intense flavors. It's not just a question of the alcohol itself: it speaks to the fact that alcohol is both a producer of flavors and one of the best solvents for them. The alcohol produced in fermentation interacts with other components in the beer recipe to produce new flavors. The alcohol fraction of the beer is also much better at dissolving flavorful compounds than the water portion.

When cooks want to extract a flavor, they generally use alcohol or fat (alcohol's chemical cousin) as a medium. Take a look at the extracts in the baking aisle next time you're in a food store. You'll notice that most of them use alcohol as the main ingredient. That's not a way to evade the liquor laws; it's because that's the best way to dissolve and deliver many flavors.

The extra work done by the yeast and the time the yeast cells were in contact with the beer also create some unique flavors.

How Much to Sip

Wine tasters typically sip between half an ounce and an ounce of wine. That won't do for tasting beer. There are lots of physical reasons that make it necessary to pour a bit heavier. In general my experience is that the lower the alcohol, the more beer you need and the less time it takes to get a sense of what a beer is about. Light, refreshing beers without much maltiness can seem insipid at first taste: you need to let them really take over your mouth in order for them to have any impact at all. Bigger beers (that is, ones with more alcohol and more intense flavor) may make their impression with a single sip and it may take minutes for the finish to work its way through your consciousness. A lot of beer bars have settled on the four-ounce (100ml) glass as the proper size for a tasting of any beer, and that seems about right.

Unlike the wine taster's bland cracker, a lightly salted pretzel may be just the right thing for in-between tastes.

Swallow or Spit

Some of the sensation of beer can only be experienced by swallowing it, but sometimes there's more beer to be tasted than can be comfortably or sanely drunk. Beer tastings haven't quite caught up with this idea and so the buckets for dumping and spitting are rare and, you should pardon my saying so, easy to miss.

Discreet spitting is mostly a wine taster's skill, but one that could be copied at a beer tasting. Probably best to practice with some beer that you wouldn't want to swallow anyway. Pull your cheeks in like a trumpet player, curl your tongue into a groove, and blow the beer out under light pressure.

With the beer spat or swallowed, pay attention to the aftertaste, or finish. Is the sensation clean or sticky? Is it sharp or sweet? Does it seem to be a natural extension of the taste of the beer or is it discordant?

Some beers, by virtue of their acidity or astringency, leave your mouth watering slightly. Our mouths are designed to water when they're hungry and conversely, the act of salivating makes us hungry and reminds us of food. Other beers leave you feeling full. Some beer will leave a disagreeable, chemical taste.

Along with the dominant flavor of the yeast, there will be other, lesser flavors in most beer, flavors created by the chemical reactions between the alcohol produced during fermentation and the native acids and phenols in the grains and hops. These secondary flavors are usually just suggestions, evocations of other tastes. Try to notice a flavor that reminds you of something else.

Vegetal, citrus and floral aromas along with bitter sensations are likely to be the product of hops. Cereal tastes and sweetness are the product of malt and flavorful grains. (Rice adds no taste at all and corn leaves an aroma reminiscent of a feed store.

Aftertaste and Afterthoughts

No matter what your tasting technique might be, there's one important thing to bear in mind:

Avoid premature evaluation!

This is the first rule of tasting. Take your time, don't look around the room to see how other people are reacting. Even though there's a certain relief involved in making up your mind, try to stay undecided as long as you can. Stay with the taste, concentrate on the play of flavors in your mouth and nose, enjoy the mystery more than you crave the solution. What you're doing is paying attention, practicing a form of awareness: this time you spend being fully attentive isn't deducted from your allotted lifespan, so luxuriate in it.

You see, the minute you make up your mind, you stop paying attention to the beer and flip over to congratulating yourself on getting it right or looking around to see if you voted with the majority. If beer tasting were a sport, the last person to make a judgment about "liking" or "not liking" would be the winner.

For what it's worth, this attitude, this sense of I'm-still-experiencing-and-I-haven't-decided may be one of beer's greatest and least-expected gifts to beer drinkers. In fact, let's give it a name: we'll call it the Taster's Prejudice. Maybe, experimentally, we could take it with us to the movies next time, or even try it out for an entire day on everything we encounter. Imagine taking that frame of mind—the sense of not being in a rush to like or dislike—on a first date.

If there's got to be a second rule, it might be to listen to what your fellow tasters say, but don't be overly persuaded by it. There is a lot of difference among people in the way they taste things. All of us have a minimum level or "threshold" at which we can detect a taste or aroma. Some experts estimate that there are at least 100 different possible odors in well-made beer. Individual thresholds for particular aromas may vary on the order of 10,000 to one. Multiply those two numbers and you see how unlikely it is that any two people will have the same experience. So while it's possible that another person's observation may help you give a name to your own, the thing that matters most is your own experience.

The Question of Quality

You may notice that beer commercials rarely talk about quality and when they do, it's only in the most general terms. Nobody ever says that they use better ingredients or that some ingredients are simply better than others. There's a reason for this modesty. The Beer Institute's Ad Code contains the following remarkable sentence:

> Beer advertising and marketing materials should never suggest that competing beers contain objectionable additives or ingredients.

What else makes great beer but great ingredients? And if some are great, aren't others necessarily, um, less great? Why shouldn't an advertiser point to the presence of corn or rice or low-grade hops in the competition's beer and its absence in its own?

There are three sources of flavor in beer. We'll learn more about them later, in chapter 4, but for now:

1. The fermentables: mostly malted barley, but also adjuncts like corn and rice sugars that are added to lower cost, sugars that are added to increase alcohol and other grains that are used to create complexity
2. The spices: mostly hops for the bitterness and the herbal aromas, but sometimes other spices come into a recipe
3. The yeast: along with making alcohol, different strains of yeast contribute their own flavors. Spicy, and pungent aromas along with all of the fruity smells that you sometimes notice come from individual yeast varieties.

What drives beer makers to produce quality beers? In essence,

Bags of sugar ready to be fermented into Victory's Golden Monkey Ale.

great beers arise from the demands of a particular market. Porter, IPA and the whole new wave of micro-brews have all been developed and refined in response to a particular consumer. On a much less sublime level, high-alcohol malt liquors, light beers and the malt-based drinks called alco-pops were also created with a particular consumer in mind.

Prejudice and Tasting Blind

Most of us are pretty insecure about our sense of taste. We don't

pay attention to it much and we don't even have much of a vocabulary to describe what we taste on those rare occasions when we are attentive. Only a real food crank would say anything like "Tasting is believing." Because we are less sure of what we're experiencing, we are more easily moved by prejudices.

There are lots of other sources of prejudice to minimize bias; we sometimes taste "blind," that is, without knowing the identity of the beer. This sounds very objective and therefore commendable, but there's less here than meets the eye. In fact, everything is evaluated in context. If we're tasting to compare similar beers, it helps to know a little something like price and the intended beer style so we know what criteria to use. The folks in the world of dog shows have this figured out and they delay or avoid judging the Kerry Blue Terriers against the Portuguese Water Dogs or either of them against the Labradoodles.

In competitive beer judging (yes, there is such a thing), the tasters know something about the beer just to avoid judging it as something that it's not.

The best thing about a beer tasting in company is that sometimes a fellow taster will mention a word or a description that helps you identify and remember a particular smell or taste. It really helps to have descriptive words because they give us a way to remember flavors. At the end of this chapter is a New Taster's Checklist. Take a copy with you when you taste and see if any of the descriptions on the list help you get a better take on the beer.

Putting It All Together

Tasting isn't just a matter of taking a beer apart and trying to see who can identify the most tastes (although I'm sure there are people who will do that). You pay attention to individual tastes and feelings because all together they make up the impression of the beer. It's a little like being a careful listener at an orchestral concert. The experienced concertgoer listens to individual instruments, but at the same time he soaks up the total harmony of all the sounds. That total sensation is what the brewer, I mean the composer, had in mind.

If the quality and harmony of flavor is what matters, you may want to think about that harmony in three ways.

Structure

Begin with the most obvious sensations: the carbonation and body in the mouth. These are easy characteristics to detect; even a tired palate can detect bubbles and thickness. Then notice some other forward qualities: sweetness, astringency (a drying or tightening sensation), alcohol, and acidity.

Beer's structural harmony comes from a balance between its body or thickness in the mouth, the soft sensations of alcohol and sugar, and the hard sensations of carbonation and acidity. If you can distinguish at least those five sensations, you'll be able to tell a well-balanced beer and better able to distinguish one that's off-kilter. A light, fresh wheat beer can be balanced and have a preponderance of acidity. An older bock beer may balance its alcohol and sweetness with strong tannins (from the husks of the grain). It's good to know that in modern beers, the carbonation is added after fermentation. The amount of sparkle is entirely up to the brewer. An aggressively carbonated (gassy) beer can hide flaws in the taste or cover up a general lack of flavor that comes from cheap ingredients, and this is a common flaw in industrial beer. (As you'll see, like Champagne, some old-fashioned beers are carbonated in the bottle.)

It's easy to get confused about the nature of sweetness in beer. Certain fruity and spicy flavors—vanilla or caramel or cider for instance—remind us of sweetness even in the absence of sugar. Real sweetness is a sensation on the tongue.

Aroma and Flavor

If the structure is harmonious, it should also fit together with the aroma and flavor. We want a mouth-filling, full-bodied beer to have a penetrating bouquet and a blockbuster flavor, and we want subtle aromas and tastes to go along with a delicate mouth feel. If there's hops bitterness, it should underline the other flavors, not overwhelm them. Once you're aware of them, it's easy to see when one of these three properties is out of proportion. Does the beer smell like it tastes? Flavor and aroma should be similar, both in intensity and character. The beer should seem like a well-balanced whole—the kind we smile and smack our lips over and that makes us ask for more.

Unharmonious beers are more likely to leave us with that puzzled look as we cock our heads and wonder what's wrong.

Finish

Finally, pay attention to the way the beer tastes after you've swallowed it. That lingering pleasant sensation called the finish is one of the characteristics that distinguishes beer from most other drinks. Some beers may leave you with a short, unpleasant little finish or leave a sour, disagreeable taste in the mouth. The best beers tell a good story all the way through and leave a finishing taste that makes you want more.

Imagine the taste of beer as a piece of music that's being played for the benefit of your sense of taste. You want the loudness of the tune to be the same all the way through. That is, the aroma should take as much of your attention as the mouth feel and the mouth feel should match the volume of the flavor on the palate and all of them should lead to a finish that's appropriate to the loudness of everything that's gone before.

Vocabulary

We're human: we love language. Sometimes language gets in the way of experience, but more often giving an experience a name helps us to remember. Name a taste and you have a way, not just to recall it but to recognize it again. Try to recall your last taste of beer: not the instance of tasting it, but the actual taste in your mouth. It's hard to do. Now give that taste a name—toasty, sour, bitter, whatever applies—and the taste almost reappears. In the case of smells and tastes, it almost seems like we can't conjure them up without their names.

Understandable as the impulse to make up a vocabulary is, beer talk is still inherently weird. We don't have a lot of words to describe tastes apart from words that are just examples of tastes.

So you sit your friend down at the bar with a glass of Guinness and a glass of Anchor Porter in front of her. She sips one and you ask:

"What does this taste like?"

"It tastes like beer."

"Oh? What does beer taste like?"

"Sort of like this."

"Okay, so what does this other beer taste like?"

"It tastes like beer too."

"So they both taste the same?"

"Not really."

This is going nowhere fast, so maybe your friend has a word or two to help. One beer is "sour," the other is "bitter." Or maybe she has a wider frame of reference and soon one beer reminds her of almond chocolate bars and the other recalls raisin toast. With practice, you can recognize lots of resemblances. This makes sense because many flavors and aromas show up in a lot of different places. But similarities alone somehow don't do justice to the taste of beer.

Beer drinkers want to say more. They want to generalize and maybe even rhapsodize, and one curious phenomenon helps them do it. The taste of beer, like the taste of wine, is easy to imagine with visual and physical terms. If you say that a beer is "heavy" or "light," most people will know what you're talking about. It's also pretty easy to grasp the difference between a "big" beer and a "little" one. To call a beer "round" is to suggest that its flavor is balanced.

Or perhaps your beer didn't deliver much flavor at all and you found it "thin," "stingy," or "empty." Add some more alcohol, protein and unfermented carbohydrates to a beer like that and you find yourself saying things like "fat" or "full" or even "generous." Not enough acidity or a deficiency of bitterness and the beer becomes "flabby."

Now it's easy to see how this vocabulary could get way out of hand. In the spirit of poetry (not to mention the alcohol in the beer itself) we might get a bit more ambitious. One beer might be a mean little fellow and another an open-handed old friend. One is lively and adventurous, another conservative and a bit dull.

The Moral of the Story

If all this makes beer tasting seem like serious business, I'm glad. But let's not turn serious into solemn. After all, we started all this to have fun and beer should lift your spirits, not be a burden to them. What I learned from tasting is that it's mostly a matter of practicing and paying attention. You can pay attention to aromas any time and to flavors often.

You may find that time spent sharpening your awareness of flavors—in beer or anything else—is time very well spent indeed. When you're done tasting, you may want to talk about what you tasted or at least make use of words to help remember the experience. One of the great things about this is the opportunity it gives you for radical truth telling. There aren't many opportunities like this: just try to think of any other areas in life where you're allowed, much less encouraged, to experience something and tell the truth.

"Does this dress make me look fat?"

"So what do you think of my book?"

"This carob tastes just like real chocolate, doesn't it?"

"That was great. Was it good for you too?"

Using the New Taster's Checklist

The New Taster's Checklist is built around questions of structure, bouquet, flavor and finish. The easiest way to begin is to describe the mouth-feel, or body, of the beer. Rate the body along a continuum from thick to thin. Ask yourself if the beer is astringent or spritzy. See if you notice any of the flavors that are in boldface type on the sheet. Make a check after that flavor.

Then see if you can refine your observation. If you "get" a fruity taste, for instance, see if you can decide what kind of fruit. There are some usual suspects like banana and apple, but you may find something else. Remember, if you taste it, it's there. When you've done that for each of the categories, you'll have a flavor profile for that beer.

This checklist doesn't ask you to assign a score. You may have seen scores or beer ratings touted on the shelf tags in liquor stores. These ratings come from the pages of magazines and websites like the *Beer Advocate* and *Ale Street News*. Thousands of beers are tasted, described, and rated, sometimes on a 100-point scale (like high school) or a 4-point scale (like college).

There's something reassuring about coming to the end of a process with a number and the assurance that a 96-point beer is better than a 92-point beer. We make use of this sort of comparison all the time, but beer may be one of the places where scores are best left behind. First, you have to remember that these are consensus ratings, averages that will downgrade an eccentric beer that might be perfect for you.

Second, not all of these tastings are blind, or even particularly nearsighted, and sometimes a reputation can influence judgments. If you're rating a beer on a website, will you be completely uninfluenced by all the ratings that went before yours? Do you think all of the other raters were unmoved by previous scores? Are you impressed or put off by a famous name? Can you taste the beer that came from a nicked bottle with an unknown label without having a predisposition to praise it or downgrade it? Good for you if you can, but most of us are made of weaker stuff.

Third, the other tasters may not value the same things that you do. Some people are hop-heads, some are taken with delicate floral aromas; others are total malt-mamas. Genuinely mature tasters try to move beyond their own predispositions to consider questions of balance (see above).

New Taster's Checklist

Body: In balance with the taste? Thick................ Thin ....
Carbonation: Proportional..................Gassy..............Flat..............

Grain
Breakfast Cereal............ Malt .... Grainy..............

Fruit
Apple .... Banana........................... Pear..................
Citrus Peel..................... Other...

Spice
Clove .... Coriander.................. Baking Spices............

Brown Sugar .... Anise............................ Juniper ....
White Pepper................ Other...

Herb
Grassy .... Walnut Skin.................. Hoppy..............
Other ....

Unpleasant Tastes

Soapy .... Moldy ....Insipid (watery)...............
Metallic .... Other...

To read some sample beer reviews go to
http://shortcourseinbeer/tastings
http://beeradvocate.com/beer/

Discussion Questions

1. Are there any other stories about food and drink that you suspect might be fakelore?

2. When you really start paying attention to taste, are there some old favorites that don't taste so good anymore?

3. What's the difference between selling beer in a world where people actually taste the stuff and selling it to a public that relates to beer on a purely symbolic level?

4. Do you think you could apply tasting techniques to other drinks? How about cola? Coffee?

5. Why do you suppose the Beer Institute, which represents all the big breweries in the country, would want to discourage talk about high- and low-quality ingredients?

6. How many advertisements can you think of that try to make a virtue out of the obvious? "Cold-filtered" beer is one; "fat-free" raisins is another. The implication in these claims is that you, the reader or viewer, are an idiot. How do you feel about that?

Chapter 3

The Question of Alcohol

When you finish this chapter, you will have
- some idea of why beer is occasionally referred to as a "social beverage"
- had some of your attitudes about alcohol reinforced and some others thoroughly undermined
- checked out the alcohol content and calorie count of some of your favorite beers
- accepted the fact that you can't really define "drunk"
- secretly congratulated yourself on the fact that you know what it means anyway
- been alerted to the forces that would snatch the beer from your hand

Alcohol is a colorless, volatile, flammable liquid. In spite of what your dictionary may say, it's not exactly flavorless. It is lighter than water and a great deal more popular. There are two reasons that drinks with alcohol have been so loved for so long.

The first and least obvious is that they were the only safe drinks, aside from boiled water, on which early, civilized humankind could rely. We talked about this in chapter 1, but this is a good place to remind ourselves that only alcohol, boiled water and a very few water sources were safe. Fruit juice, if it existed at all, turned itself into wine because of the yeasts in the air.

Only wine, which does not support—and often restricts—any bacteria harmful to man, and beer, which was scalded as it was made, were safe. People and cities that made or bought wine and beer were healthier than those that didn't. In places where the grape vines didn't grow, a boiled extract of sprouted barley grains was used. The boiling made the drink safer than the water from which it was made. Sprouted barley, sometimes called malt, contains a fair amount of starch. When this starch is converted to sugar and extracted by soaking the grain in hot water, you have a liquid that will ferment into beer in the presence of airborne yeast. This beer probably didn't resemble the beverage that we know today, but it was certainly safer to drink than water.

Even in colonial America

The family privy and the local well were likely to be too close together. An advertisement offering a well-reputed Boston tavern for sale listed as all in the same yard stable, pump, five pigsties and one house of office [privy].

J.C. Furans

The connection of wine and beer with health remains strong today. Drinking water is still not universally safe. (With a few exceptions, potable municipal water supplies did not appear until the seventeenth century. It was also that century that saw the introduction of the stimulant alternatives to alcohol: coffee, tea and chocolate.) More importantly, many people connect the moderate consumption of wine and beer with a healthy and civilized life. There is significant evidence that they are right.

There are other ways to make drinking water safe. If fuel is available, water can be boiled, but the case for boiling isn't obvious unless some flavorings are added. In East Asia, civilizations relied as much on teas as Western Asian and Mediterranean cities did on wine and beer. The cultivation of grapes and grain for alcoholic beverages remained part of civilization's toolkit for reasons that went beyond sanitation and into a different realm of hygiene.

Alcohol's other virtue is that it has a mild and pleasantly intoxicating effect. Early physicians may have praised wine and beer as medicine for the body, but it was Socrates who, as Hugh Johnson reminds us, spoke of drink's ability to "lull the cares of the mind to

A copper kettle in a community brewery in Berchtesgaden, Bavaria.

rest and … pleasantly invite us to agreeable mirth." One of the first questions people ask about a beer is its (alcoholic) "strength." What a peculiar expression! You might want to know the concentration of salt in your soup or the amount of cholesterol in your salad dressing, but when it comes to alcohol, you ask "how strong?"

Well, the general answer is easy. When measured by volume, most of the beer in the world is between 3.5 and 6 percent alcohol. There are mild beers with less alcohol and even beers with less than 0.5 percent alcohol that are allowed to call themselves non-alcoholic. There are stronger beers too, and even a few that surpass the 12–14 percent of wine.

The alcohol in any beverage comes from the sugar. In the case of beer the sugar is derived from malt. The more sugar you start out with, the more there is for the yeast to consume and the more alcohol you'll have when you're done. It's worth noting that since alcohol is much lighter than water, the question of "how much" has two different answers.

The first answer is a matter of percentage of alcohol by weight, and is the one preferred by brewers for its direct relation to the brewing process and its ease of calculation. The second answer is by the percentage of the total volume and is preferred by collectors of the excise tax. It's also the one that appears on beer labels as ABV. To calculate the percentage by volume, brewers just multiply the percentage by weight by 1.25.

Attenuation is a nice way of referring to the disappearance of sugar and its replacement by alcohol during fermentation. Apparent attenuation is the amount of specific gravity that the beer seems to have lost between its unfermented and fermented states, and thus an indirect (and approximate) measure of the alcohol level in the beer. Some microbrewers prefer to cite the Apparent Attenuation because it seems more refined and draws attention away from the alcohol level. All the alcohol concentrations given in this book are percentages by volume. (% ABV)

Just Say Know

The specific answer to the question "how much alcohol is in this particular beer" is much harder to give. In the United States, beers were not allowed to proclaim their alcohol content after 1935. The general feeling is that if they did, weak-spined alcohol-suckers like you would rush to buy the most alcoholic beers. Brewers, crazed with greed, would then start raising the alcohol content of their products in a blatant appeal to the induced unconsciousness market. Eventually, alcohol percentages would become part of brand names and advertising slogans. (Drink Schultz Thirteen! The first one is way too many!) Eventually, every man, woman and child in the country would wake up in the morning, chug a pint of 20 percent alcohol beer and fall into a stupor. Factories would close, schools would empty and American farmland would be taken over by kudzu and deer ticks.

If you think I'm exaggerating the danger, just look at the horrible situation in Europe, where crude alcohol levels have been placed right out on the front of beer bottles for years (it's called "frontal crudity").

Of course, keeping you ignorant of how much alcohol is in a beer also keeps you ignorant of how little is in it and so acts as an impediment to moderation. But that's probably just a coincidence (see the discussion of Prohibition in chapter 1).

In 1987 Coors Brewing Company sued the government, saying that the Federal Law was unconstitutional. In October of 1992, a Federal court overturned the law. Subsequently, a few products from Anheuser-Busch have been released in test markets with ALC/VOL displayed on can or bottle label. Many breweries do list % ABV on the label, but as of this writing, it's strictly voluntary. In some states, there are specific regulations. In North Carolina, any malt beverage containing more than 6% ABV has to show a label clearly indicating the alcohol content.

Recently, an unlikely coalition has proposed a new regulation. Brewers would have to list the alcohol and calorie content as well as any ingredients that might provoke an allergic reaction in an unwitting customer. They would also have to list the conventional Nutrition Information that you find on the side of a granola box and an advisory about the number of "standard" drinks in the container. It sounds harmless enough, but small brewers would have to pay for an expensive analysis with every seasonal or occasional beer they brewed. It's an especially silly burden, because we know in advance that beer (and wine and spirits too) traditionally have no fat, no protein and none of the common allergens.

So who's behind this? On one side is a neo-prohibitionist outfit called the Center for Science in the Public Interest. Allied with them is Diageo, owner of the Guinness brand and some of the most prestigious distilled spirits in the world. CSPI is hoping, according to a spokesman, "to reduce the problems associated with drinking." Diageo, on the other hand, uses its website to promote parity between spirits and beer: same alcohol, different vehicles. Apparently this spirits giant feels that a statement about the "equivalence" of beer and spirits will be to the advantage of spirits. Beer has been making strange bedfellows for years, but this pairing is remarkable: one side hopes to decrease consumption of alcohol, the other is trying to increase it. Somebody's going to look gullible here. Stay tuned.

American brewers fought once before for the right to list calories. In 1967 Rheingold Breweries introduced Gablinger's, the first beer that acknowledged that drinking might make you fat. The Federal Alcohol Administration Act then prohibited the listing of calories on beer containers because that would constitute a health claim. But the Food and Drug Administration required the listing of calories on any product that made a dietary claim. Rheingold had to sue for the right.

If you want to know the calories in your beer, the easiest way is to go to this website:
http://www.realbeer.com

Alcohol in beer plays a critical role in the flavor and charm of the drink. The improvement that it causes is not directly related to the alcohol itself: alcohol has only a slight, sweet flavor. The difference comes partly from the aromatic flavor components of beer that are created by fermentation and partly from the mouth feel of alcohol. The higher the alcohol level, the greater the production of these flavors.

The aromatic components of hops are resins, which are more soluble in alcohol than in water. Beers that rely on hops aroma or that use dry hopping to enhance bouquet are more effective when their alcohol level is higher.

Some brewers take advantage of this effect in their low-alcohol product by using a technique called high gravity brewing in which a beer is fermented at a higher-than-intended alcohol level and then brought down to drinking strength with water.

Alcohol and the Human Body

Alcohol gets into the human body from all parts of the gastrointestinal tract largely by simple diffusion into the blood; however, the small intestine is by far the most efficient region of the gastrointestinal tract for alcohol absorption because of its very large surface area. Alcohol is absorbed into your bloodstream and forwarded on to your brain through tissues in your mouth, stomach and small intestine. If you're fasting, the intestine does about 75 percent of the work thanks to its larger surface area. Alcohol in the blood quickly travels throughout the body.

Alcohol and the Brain

Alcohol affects the brain with a strict attention to the class system. The higher centers get beat up first. Sensory information gets scrambled, thinking gets, um, disordered, and then voluntary muscular movements become a tidge uncoordinated. After the inner philosopher is trashed, alcohol moves on to rough up the poet. People become subject to exaggerated emotions and memory loss. With your inner Robert Frost dead and gone, more alcohol (that is, a higher concentration in the blood) goes after the animal inside you. You know that test where they ask you to close your eyes and touch your finger to your nose? The ability that's being tested is mediated through a part of your brain called the cerebellum, and you can usually do it smoothly. Turn off the cerebellum and the movements become jerky and uncertain (as do you). These delicate movements are like the ones that we use to control our balance, and so the cerebellum-pickled drinker may start falling down. The lusty animal is affected too. Alcohol depresses the areas of the hypothalamus that coordinate sexual endocrine functions. So although sexual behavior may increase, sexual performance declines. In men, this is the so-called "whisky-dick" effect. If for some reason, you get to this point and still manage to keep on drinking, you may be saved by the body's natural tendency to fall asleep. This tendency is also referred to less kindly as passing out, and indulging in it more than once can get you banned from some very nice taverns. If Morpheus, Sleep God Brother of Death, doesn't come to your rescue, or if you manage to bypass him by swallowing tidal amounts of alcohol, then breathing, heart rate and body temperature centers are affected. Blood pressure can drop and breathing can stop and your organ donor card and emergency instructions can become effective. Be aware that drinking yourself to death gives the rest of us a bad name.

Getting Rid of It

Fortunately, the same body that took all that alcohol in is capable of hauling it out, mostly by metabolizing it in the liver. A small amount is expelled in the breath, saliva, urine, feces and sweat. (A small amount is also excreted in breast milk, although if you're producing breast milk and drinking lots of alcohol, perhaps you should be reading some other book.) Except for the possible acceleration caused by jumping into a sauna or running a marathon, most of us eliminate alcohol at a steady rate. There is some variability among people in their ability to dilute and get rid of what they paid to take in. The big differences are the water content and fat content of the body. Practically, this means that:

- The less you weigh, the more you will be affected by a given amount of alcohol. Bigger people have more blood and more tissue and so the alcohol is diluted over a larger volume.
- The more muscular you are, the less affected you'll be. Fat doesn't have much water (duh), and muscular souls have more blood vessels and more water-absorbing tissue. Watch out for

the body builders at the beer tasting.

- Gender counts. Women have a triple whammy here. They tend to have smaller bodies with higher body fat percentages, which means less watery tissue. They also tend to process alcohol through the liver more slowly because of a lower level of an alcohol-digesting hormone.
- Age matters too. Older people eliminate alcohol more slowly, although the effects of this may be mitigated by the so-called "practice effect." This is part of what's behind the common observation that old drunks can handle their liquor better.
- Food can slow the absorption of alcohol through several mechanisms. Not only is alcohol slowed in its entrance to the small intestine, but the lower concentrations that result speed up the rate of elimination.

There's more, of course. Arousal can slow the passage of alcohol from the stomach to the intestine and the person looking for a pre-determined level of buzz may fail to reach it with the first few doses and then overshoot. Anxiety can increase the rate of absorption and so can carbonation and even artificial sweeteners. So, let's lay off the aspartame-enhanced malt liquor when we're really really tense, okay?

Just What Do We Mean by "Drunk"?

A person whose blood contains more than 0.1 percent alcohol is considered legally drunk in most jurisdictions. In many European countries, the standard for judging a driver to be "under the influence of alcohol" is much lower—from 0.05 to 0.08 percent. In Japan, any alcohol at all in a driver's blood is illegal. These specific numbers are necessary for the law and reassuring to the rest of us. Add to this the fact that we may have some personal experience of the matter, and we end up thinking that we know what "drunk" is.

But drunkenness is far from a single, simple thing. It's a continuum that involves emotions, perception, consciousness and behavior.

At one end of the scale is a pleasant lightening of the spirit, the sort of uplift that has made the drink after work a ritual for so many. At the other end, there is a complete breakdown of all the human functions. In between, there are an infinite number of states along each of those dimensions: some of the combinations are pleasant, others exalted, and some others purely miserable. As any bartender or cocktail waitress can tell you, a person drunk is remarkably different from that same person sober, and there are many, many different ways for a person to be drunk.

The shift from sober to drunk is as drastic to the person undergoing it as it is to someone observing him or her. Shy people become outgoing, timid folks become foolhardy, inhibited souls discover their libidinous side. If drunkenness were not such a common experience and one so often depicted, we would be astonished by it and beg for an explanation.

Any attempt to explain inebriation leaves us with more questions about the idea of explanation than it does answers about being drunk. A glib explanation is that people get drunk because alcohol disinhibits the brain. Does this explain it? Not hardly. Unless you have a deep understanding of brain physiology, that's just another set of words for the same thing. (You might as easily say that the beer fairies came along and stole your IQ.)

We're easily duped into accepting this sort of circular thinking as an explanation because, as citizens of our own times, we have a certain faith in the material dimension of things. We're right to believe: rigorous material explanations make for good engineering. But before this belief came along in, let's say the seventeenth century, what kind of explanation might have occurred to people who wondered just what drunkenness was?

Forget what you know for a minute, and imagine that you're drinking some alcohol-enhanced drink for the first time. Let's say that you live in a world with few physical comforts and a badly stocked medicine chest. What would it be like to get drunk for the first time? For most people, drinking probably just lessened the daily dose of pain and made them feel less bad. This "feeling good" must have seemed like a surprise visit to another place, a divine place.

Remember, the notion of alcohol as some specific property of a drink is a fairly new idea. Distilling the "spirit" of wine only began in the thirteenth century and the word *alcohol* comes into existence thanks to Paracelsus, the physician/alchemist of Salzburg in the seventeenth century. Giving a name to the ingredient that makes one drunk created a step back, a kind of abstraction. Before that, there was only the mystery of the drink itself.

What to make of that mystery? In much of the ancient world it seemed like a gift from the gods. The ancient Greeks were not very fond of their gods. They, (the gods, not the Greeks) were a nasty bunch. But one of them was different: Dionysus, the god of wine. He entered your body when you drank wine, you could feel his presence and it was a good one.

But Dionysus was not completely a warm fuzzy teddy bear. The adjective "Dionysian" frequently modifies the noun "frenzy." The festivals in his honor were known for their wild dancing and uninhibited behavior.

Greece died after Alexander, and the Romans inherited the bones. They also inherited important aspects of Greek drinking culture, particularly the notion of drink and its consequences as visitations from the divine.

In Rome, Dionysus becomes Bacchus, and he appears in murals and mosaics with a halo of leaves and sitting as an infant on the knee of his virgin mother, Semele.

But what about the gods of beer?

The Greeks built their civilization on the trade in wine, and Romans, like modern Italians, were wine drinkers first. But beer had a role at the fringes of the world where grapes didn't grow. There was a Greco-Roman god of beer. He is Silenus (fat, bald and drunk) and he makes a pointed cultural contrast to the pretty Dionysus and is a minor figure.

In the Egyptian world, Osiris is the god of agriculture who taught people how to brew. There is also a profound connection between the importance of beer and its inebriating effect in the story of the goddess Hathor. In a tale that parallels the story of the Flood, the god Ra punishes rebellious mankind by creating a bloodthirsty goddess, Hathor. Alarmed at the extent of her destruction and taking pity on mankind, he orders beer to be brewed and mixed with red ochre, and uses it to flood the place where Hathor is to continue her killing. The murderous goddess sees the lake of blood:

> Then she laughed with joy, and her laughter was like the roar of a lioness hungry for the kill. Thinking that it was indeed blood, she stooped and drank. Again and yet again she drank, laughing with delight; and the strength of the beer mounted to her brain, so that she could no longer slay.
>
> At last she came reeling back to where Ra was waiting; that day she had not killed even a single man.
>
> Then Ra said: "You come in peace, sweet one." And her name was changed to Hathor, and her nature was changed also to the sweetness of love and the strength of desire. And henceforth Hathor laid low men and women only with the great power of love. But forever after her priestesses drank in her honor of the beer of Heliopolis colored with the red ochre of Elephantine when they celebrated her festival each New Year.

In the story, the power of the beer is that it turns wrath into love.

More importantly, the Babylonian goddess Ninkasi is herself a brewer.

When you pour out the filtered beer of the collector vat,

It is [like] the onrush of Tigris and Euphrates.
Ninkasi, you are the one who pours out the filtered beer of the collector vat,
It is [like] the onrush of Tigris and Euphrates.
Hymn to Ninkasi

Alcohol and Attitude

Ask anyone who's ever tended a bar or nursed a hangover: alcohol may have gods, but it is not always a blessing. Sitting at the same table with the lightened spirits and occasional hilarity of good-natured drinking is the destructive nightmare of the out-of-control drunk.

There are even some people who distrust alcohol for its virtues. These are folks who are threatened by that lighter, looser state of consciousness in themselves and other people, the fear that the jolly poet is really the lecherous pirate in disguise. One person's lightened spirit becomes someone else's terrorizing demon. You probably don't need me to tell you that people drinking beer—or anything else—are more likely to be boisterous and to act out sexually. They're also more likely to be aggressive, obnoxious or deficient in good judgment. This last effect is sometimes jokingly referred to as Beer Goggles. One particularly cruel bumper sticker says: BEER. Helping ugly people get laid since 1842.

All culture is built on some sort of inhibition, and if your idea of goodness is based on a heavy-duty set of inhibitions, then the moderately disinhibiting effect of alcohol is likely to be very threatening. People who have come to be afraid of their own impulses are often also repelled by them and find themselves wanting to wipe out or at least disguise them in others.

Any useful understanding of alcohol starts with acknowledging the feelings, attitudes and knowledge you acquired at home. After you acknowledge those feelings, it's good to remember the context in which we drink today. In America, we're still pretty much car-crazy. In more tolerant contexts, people more frequently walk from place to place. A certain unsteadiness on the street may be amusing, but the same impairment at the wheel can be deadly.

> No account of the pleasures of beer can sidestep the question of the horror caused by drunken drivers. According to the Centers for Disease Control, over 17,000 people died in alcohol-related automobile accidents in 2007. In spite of the fact that almost three-quarters of those convicted of drunk driving violations are alcoholics, it's a bad idea for anyone to mix even moderate beer consumption and driving. Designated drivers and good public transit systems are a beer lover's best friends. If you have a choice, drink beer in Vienna and bottled water in Los Angeles.

In the United States, alcohol is the subject of much passionate debate and very little rational reflection. By some estimates, a third of American adults do not drink anything with alcohol. For some it is a matter of religious belief: Mormons, Muslims and Hindus do not drink. Members of some Christian sects construe even the wine-friendly Bible as forbidding drinking. In addition, there are millions of people who believe that their personal problems have their roots in an uncontrollable addiction to alcohol. This last group has brewed up a large "alcoholism industry." Look up the word "Alcoholism" in an American phone directory and you will see a list of organizations that derive their reason for being from the perception of alcohol as a threat.

On the other hand (there is always, in discussion of alcohol, another hand), recent studies have shown with an amazing regularity that people who drink beer and wine moderately and regularly are physically and emotionally healthier in every sense than those who drink too little or those who drink too much. These research results get a lot less publicity than do the dueling, contradictory and less useful results of studies about the health effects of other foods. Results showing the benign effects of drinking have, of course, been deliberately ignored by the alcoholism industry.

We should also pause for a moment to consider the curious reverse snobbery about beer. Members of the American working class who are of northern European or African descent drink beer to the exclusion of wine. Putting aside Italian and French immigrants, their perception is that beer, particularly cheap industrial beer, is the drink of the common man. Many people who should know better scorn beer for the same reason. In fact, although certain foods have come to be identified with certain social classes, taste itself is above class. Some beer is noble, some is not.

In the face of all this high-key and often very primitive passion, it is sometimes difficult for reasonable voices to be heard. Tolerance and moderation are inherently less spectacular than absolutism. In the matter of alcohol, as in so many other matters, these two virtues are the ones that count.

Here's another no-surprise: for many college students, being away from home and having virtually unlimited access to alcoholic beverages for the first time is an occasion for some pretty immoderate behavior. It doesn't help that many students have no experience of beer (or any other alcohol) as a part of a moderate enjoyment. It's always easy for the grown-ups on a college campus to tell who grew up in a family of moderate drinkers and who didn't. The kids who drink moderately are smiling on Monday morning: the apprentice drunks and the glumly abstemious are not. If excess drinking only cost the occasional freshman hangover, we could pass over college drunkenness as a mere rite of passage. But in fact, even in the Eden of college life, immoderate drinking can exact a very high price. Unwanted pregnancy, STDs, date rape, fatal accidents and other calamities can all be the outcome of too much alcohol.

So how does a person learn moderation? The best advice I ever heard for novice drinkers was wonderfully simple: Drink like you've been doing it all your life and like you will be doing it forever. Imagine that it's fun and tasty and no big deal, and then it will be. For the parents of kids who are not yet drinking, the best advice I ever heard was: Show your kids what moderation looks like and you'll never have to tell them. For college administrators, the best advice might be to provide high-profile occasions on which moderate drinking is the norm. My genteel old alma mater used to host a "Dean's tea" every semester for everyone who made Dean's List. It was an afternoon event and everyone, faculty, deans and students alike, had a glass or two of sherry.

Moderation

In case you hadn't noticed, unrestricted drinking and drunkenness have fallen out of favor again. We find ourselves with a shrill and uneasy battle between people of good will holding these two positions:

- Drinking any drink with alcohol in it is sinful or unhealthy or irresponsible. Drinkers are hurting themselves and threatening the rest of us. In fact, any explicit attempt to control the nature of one's own consciousness subverts natural law and true religion.
- Drinking is fun and one person's drinking is none of anyone else's business. The government is not entitled to tax or regulate one person's pleasures more punitively than another's.

Neither of these positions is particularly moderate, but let's not rush to pronounce an anathema on either or both of these camps. Moderation is a Johnny-come-lately virtue, a habit that has to be learned and that has no great tradition behind it. In fact moderate drinking is a recent and necessary next step in human development.

Why drink moderately? Because there is really no sane alternative. Unrestricted drunkenness may have been a scandal in the seventeenth century; in our times it's dangerous and intolerable. The drunk in George II's England could start a fight, perhaps kill somebody. Today's drunk can pass out at the switch of the power plant or careen down the freeway and take out a school bus.

If unrestricted drinking is unthinkable, so is Prohibition in both its disguised and blatant forms. If America's disastrous experience described above was not enough to prove the point, one could turn to the British Gin Act of 1736, which managed to quadruple the consumption of locally distilled gin in a mere seven years by prohibiting the import of liquor.

More important than that is the fact that drinks with alcohol add to the civilized pleasures of a world without much civilization and with precious little pleasure. Prohibitionists are trying to take their lack of culture and their joylessness out on the rest of us.

Moderation is not only sound policy, it's good sense too. The medical evidence is overwhelming: moderate enjoyment of drinks with alcohol adds to a healthy life. But drinking without getting drunk only makes sense if the drinking is a reward in itself. Good beer is the drink of moderation because it's delicious. We'll have some practical advice about moderation later, but for now let's just note that good beer (and good wine) make moderation as pleasant as it is virtuous.

Moderation and Ambivalence

These observations about alcohol and moderation are not exactly new. They seem to have been dueling almost as long as alcohol has been around, although the debate heats up as more potent alcoholic drinks become available in the 1600s. In a few societies, one point of view has temporarily overridden the other, but the most common condition has been a kind of armed truce between the two views and the people who represent them. The Hebrews, although they made wine the material of every sacrament, were still a bit conflicted:

Wine is a scoffer, beer a roisterer; He who is muddled by them will not grow wise.
Proverbs, XX, 1

Give beer to the unfortunate and wine to those with heavy hearts.
Proverbs, XXXI, 6

If you want to play search-a-quote, you can assemble similar pairs of epigrams from many other cultures.

Two things are obvious after the beer lovers and the naysayers have been heard from:

The beer lovers have all the good lines.

God has a brown voice, as soft and full as beer.
Anne Sexton

There can't be good living where there is not good drinking.
Benjamin Franklin

I have taken more out of alcohol than alcohol has taken out of me.
Winston Churchill

The "solution" that most thinkers recommend is the middle ground of moderation.

So what, or more specifically, how much, is moderate? Keep in mind that we're looking for a way to enjoy the benefits of beer without becoming a victim of the costs. The Attic Greeks specified three drinks as the righteous dose: the first for health, the second for companionship, and the third for sleep. Coincidentally, one modern standard of moderation is one drink an hour, which works out to twelve ounces of 5% beer.

That one drink an hour is about the rate at which your liver can reduce alcohol to sugar. Anything above that goes into your blood and brain as alcohol. It's this "excess" alcohol spilling out of an overworked liver that makes us drunk. One drink is a twelve-ounce bottle of beer and one beer an hour is, with food, a fairly civilized pace of consumption. One might even call it moderate.

The Bottom Line

Beer has alcohol and alcohol has a central and powerful place in the imaginations of most people. It is the devil and it is a god. It's the food of angels and madmen. It is the source of tremendous benefits and we pay a fairly high price for them. It is easy to love alcohol and only a bit harder to hate it.

Somewhere between those two extremes there's a place where we recognize that the good or evil in things may not be in the things themselves, but in us. That's a place called moderation.

Discussion Questions

1. How successful would you be in founding a church of Bacchus in the US? Do you think the Post Office would ever give your church its own stamp? How about Hathor or Ninkasi?
2. Does the War on Alcohol of 1919-1933 remind you at all of the current War on Drugs? Are there any lessons to be learned from one to apply to the other?
3. What do you think about the idea that restricting access to alcohol discourages moderation? Is there really a forbidden fruit effect?
4. If you called your first beer of the evening "h" and the second beer "u" and the third beer "n" and the fourth beer "g," by the time you got to that fourth beer you'd be "hung." Suppose you

called the fifth beer "over." Do you think that might persuade you to put off ordering that fifth beer? No? Why not?

Chapter 4

How is Beer Made?

When you finish this chapter, you will

- have a good idea about how that delicious beer got to your glass
- appreciate the choices that make one beer taste different from another
- understand that today's beers are both ancient and new
- perhaps be tempted to make your own beer or cider

Yeast and Fermentation

The truth is that we don't make beer at all. Yeast makes beer by a natural biological process called fermentation. What we get to do is help the process along.

Fermentation works like this: Yeast eats sugar that's been dissolved in water and gives off alcohol and carbon dioxide (CO_2).

Fermentation also creates chemicals called esters, which are volatile flavor compounds. Volatile means that they evaporate easily and so make themselves available to your nose. They are formed by the combination of organic acids and the alcohols formed during fermentation. Most of the fruity aromas of beer, (and indeed, many of the fruity aromas of fruit), come from esters. Yeast, its diet and its waste products are the heart of making wine and bread too. In bread making, the alcohol formed is evaporated in the oven; in wine making, the CO_2 is released into the air. In traditional beer making, both products are preserved. Alcoholic fermentation has been around for a long time and any sugary solution that hasn't been protected against yeast will support it. There is scarcely a sweet liquid that has not been fermented at one time or another in the pre-industrial world. Low-alcohol drinks have been prepared from bananas, apples, beetroot, birch and maple sap, honey, sugar cane juice, oranges and tomatoes. With a little more effort, the starch of squash, corn, millet, sorghum and rice have all been converted to sugar and then fermented out.

In places where alcohol has been forbidden, modern folks have made alcoholic beverages from raisins, table sugar, lemon juice and tea. In fact, as long as the sweet liquid has the right vitamins for the survival of the yeast (both yeast and nutrient can be purchased at any wine makers' supply) you can ferment just about anything.

> "The mass becomes heated and swells; carbonic acid gas is disengaged, and the sugar disappears and is replaced by alcohol." Louis Pasteur

We could make alcohol from sweet colas, from pancake syrup, from fruit punch, corn syrup or crushed and macerated breakfast cereal. We could also use the expensive sugar from apricots, cherries or maple trees. We could, but we don't. Instead, we ferment the cheapest possible sugar, the stuff made by breaking down the starch in grain or tubers. Barley was a quickly maturing cereal crop whose starch could be converted to sugar simply by sprouting the grains. Until ethanol from corn became valuable as fuel and caused the price of corn to go up, corn was a source of even cheaper alcohol.

The following is, like most group biographies, a simplified version. There are lots of variations, some of which are explained when we discuss various beer styles.

The sugar that we need for fermentation in beer making is stored in a matrix of starchy carbohydrates and protein. Before it can be fermented, the starch has to be converted to sugar. The conversion involves a bit of deception. First the grain is warmed and dampened.

Extra roasting time and higher temperatures make the malted barley on the right darker.

Large piles of grain are formed and turned over at regular intervals: the sprouting, or malting as it's known in the trade, converts the barley's hard starch into a soft soluble one. It also develops a few useful enzymes. Before these sprouts can be snapped up by organic salad makers looking for a new frontier, they are baked or kilned. The heat of baking kills the sprout but leaves the starch and the starch-breaking enzymes intact.

Malted barley is also the source of proteins that are converted by the yeast into both flavor compounds and head-retaining compounds. Beers that are made with a low proportion of malted barley have to rely on other protein sources with lyrical names like *propylene glycol alginate* to keep the head on your glass of beer. In general, those beers aren't concerned much with flavor.

Kinds of Malt

There are two kinds of barley malt: specialty and traditional. Traditional, or brewers' malt, is a complex, relatively natural product that contains everything needed to make a fermented drink. Along with the starch, there's sugar, enzymes produced by sprouting, and nutrients.

Specialty malts are exaggerated versions of brewers' malt. One characteristic or the other is enhanced to emphasize particular flavors, colors or functions. So in each stage of the malting process—steeping, germination and kilning—some aspect of the process is altered.

Hot temperatures and longer times in the kiln decrease enzymes and darken colors. Toasted and nut-like flavors may develop.

Specialty malts are made with a great deal of attention in small batches and are much more expensive than brewers' malts. They are usually used in small amounts to nudge a beer's flavor, color or texture in a particular direction.

Black Patent

Intense carbonized, burnt caramel, biscuity, woody flavor; intense aroma can be used in porter or stout. Its flavor can be harsh, so black patent malt usually makes no more than 3 percent of the total malt bill.

Biscuit

This malt gives a bakeshop aroma and flavor and will tint a beer a garnet brown color. All the enzymes have been inactivated, so it must be mashed with malts having excess enzymatic power. Used in lagers, especially dark ones, where more malt flavor without extra sweetness is called for.

Carapils (Dextrin Malt)

This malt adds body as well as helping to stabilize the head on the finished beer. It does not change the color of the finished beer. Carapils must be mashed with basic malt, due to its lack of enzymes.

Chocolate Malt
This is the most lightly roasted of the black malts. Small amounts add a red color and roasted flavor.

Crystal
Crystal resembles Carapils, but it adds a distinct sweetness. Crystal malt comes in a variety of colors, from pale to dark.

Munich
Intensely malty flavor and a medium amber color. Usually used in Festbiers, Bocks and Pale Ales.

Special B
A well roasted dark and raisiny malt whose plum-like character shows up when high concentrations are used. You can taste it in Belgian beers, especially Abbey Doubles.

Malting
This is where the brewer's choices begin and where the whole process starts to sound a lot like a conventional recipe. A short, cool kilning makes a pale, light-flavored malt; longer, hotter roasting adds a toasty flavor and darker color to the grain. Extremely high temperatures can also create unfermentable sugars called dextrins, which give a beer body. It's also possible to dry the grain over smoky peat fires. The beer that's made from that malt might just—if it's made from malt from a single source—end up being distilled, aged and served as a single-malt Scotch whisky. Wheat can also be malted, although the process is more delicate because wheat sprouts are more easily broken as the grain is turned. Most wheat beers are made with unmalted wheat and rely

Scrubbing the mash tun.

on the enzymes of sprouted barley to turn their starch to sugar. To convert the soft starch to fermentable sugar, the grain is crushed and soaked in water in a large vessel called a mash tun. The actual mashing involves heating the water to about 150F and letting the grain soak for an hour or more. The heating activates enzymes that make vitamins for the yeast and contribute to the beer's head. It also kick-starts the enzymes that will convert the soft starch into fermentable sugar. The fermentable sugar dissolves into the hot water and the color of the grain is extracted. At the same time, protein-attacking enzymes go to work, breaking long, insoluble protein chains into amino acids that will later nourish the yeast and add body to the beer. During mashing, the brewer makes choices about how thoroughly to convert starch to sugar and how much protein to leave behind. Both unconverted starch and leftover proteins contribute to the body of the finished beer. In the simplest process, the water and grain meet all at once in a single step called infusion mashing, which is frequently compared to the making of a gigantic pot of tea. Decoction mashing, the more controlled type, has the water introduced at a fairly low temperature and the mixture held there for a while. Some of the mash is then withdrawn and boiled and added back to the mash tun. The mash rests at the new, higher temperature for a while and then more is drawn off and boiled and added until the final mash temperature is reached. Decoction mashing is more efficient and better able to extract intense malty flavors.

Mashing sprouted grain isn't the only way to convert starch to sugar. In the Americas, Inca women made a paste by chewing corn and spitting the paste into cooked corn. The same enzymes that work in saliva to make grain more digestible make the cornstarch into fermentable sugar. You may be as surprised as I am that no modern brewer has tried to replicate the process: there are so many intriguing possibilities for label design and marketing campaigns. Just the advertising allure of using celebrity spit . . . In Asia, brewers make use of a mold—aspergillum—which readily grows on cooked rice. The rice/mold mixture is mixed with more rice, and yeast is added. The fermentation and the conversion to sugar happen simultaneously to produce *sake*. See chapter 7 for a bit more about sake.

Wort

Making sugary water called wort (pronounced wert) from nothing but a hot water soak of malted barley is the standard procedure for making most high-quality beers. Some brewers may use other sources of starch or sugar. These are called "adjuncts." Wheat and certain specialty sugars add to the complexity of the taste of beer.

Corn and rice are used as adjuncts to replace barley and lower the cost of the product. Rice adds no flavor in beer brewing, but corn leaves a distinct flavor that you can sample by tasting the cheapest beer you can find. Some tasters find that there is a definite vegetable and pop-corn taste, others mention the lip-smacking aroma of bean sprouts.

These days, most brewers get their water from municipal water supplies. They filter it and then add back the appropriate amounts of minerals for the style of beer that they brew. One big brewer who cites a particular mountain range, trucks its beer across country in concentrated form to be diluted in regional bottling plants. If brewers brag about their source of water, it should suggest to the consumer that maybe they don't have much else to brag about.

Brick sheathing around the brew kettle saves energy.

Hops vines outside Philadelphia Brewing Company.

The wort is moved to a different kettle and boiled. Boiling kills off any wild yeasts or bacteria that might try to feed on the sugar. (This is the "brewing" that gives you your brew.) Boiling drives off some ill-smelling compounds from the malt and reduces the volume of protein that makes it to the fermenter. It also extracts flavor and aroma from the hops. The hops plant grows all over the beer-making world in dozens of different varieties. Adding hops at the beginning of the boil allows the extraction of relatively insoluble alpha acids that contribute beer's characteristic bitterness.

Hops may also be added at any time after the boil is over. This is called dry-hopping. The cooler temperatures involved preserve the aroma of the hops without extracting any more alpha acids. Each variety of hops has its own distinctive aroma and bittering capacity, and a beer may contain more than one kind of hops.

Hops Varieties

Historically, hops are a relatively recent addition to beer. Hopped beers were resisted in England, and the first hop vines weren't grown there until 1524. Irish monastic breweries used gentian and brewing monasteries elsewhere in Europe made a mixture of herbs called gruit or groot. In America, when the frontier overreached the hops supply, spruce twigs and yarrow were used to provide some liveliness (unseasoned beer tends to be dull tasting stuff).

From a brewer's perspective, there are three types of hops.

Bittering hops

These provide a high concentration of alpha acids and give beer its bitter taste. Recently, American hops growers have been breeding varieties with ever higher alpha acid concentrations so that the needs of brewers can be satisfied while using fewer acres of plants. Bittering hops rarely get mentioned on labels, but they have names like Galena, Eroica and Nugget.

Aroma hops

These are the hops that give the perfume that floats above the rim of your glass and lures you to your first sip. Typical aromas are floral, spicy and fruity, with citrus being common.

Combination hops

These are really aromatic hops that have enough bitterness to need no supplementation. The Noble hops mentioned below are good examples.

Here are some whose aromas you may notice:

Cascades is aggressively citrusy with a floral hint. It has become almost standard in American versions of English ales. Beautifully expressed in Sierra Nevada Pale Ale, grotesquely overused elsewhere.

Fuggles has a spicy, woodsy aroma and is a staple in English ales. Beginning homebrewers sometimes name their dogs and cats "Fuggles."

Kent Goldings is another traditional English ale hop that can be used alone as a combination bittering/aroma variety: popular with homebrewers.

Hallertauer* is a German variety with a pleasant, grassy aroma.

Saaz* is the classic Pilsner hops. Taste it in its purest form in Czechvar or Urquell and you'll notice references to it in every other pilsner you drink. Herbal, spicy and clean.

Spalt* is from the Bavarian town of the same name; taste in any of the Ayinger lagers, showing a mild but spicy aroma.

Tettnanger* is a German relative of Saaz. High-yielding and popular in American Pilsners.

*These varieties together are known as the **Noble Hops**. Taste them all together in the American Prima Pils.

Some of the principal ingredients of gruit were themselves mildly intoxicating: heather, sweet gale, mugwort, yarrow, hops itself and the truly frightening marsh Labrador tea. The mixtures varied, some being more soporific and others more arousing. Hops won out over gruit in part for political reasons. Gruit mixtures were cultivated and packaged from monastic gardens: in some places, monasteries enjoyed exclusive rights to the sale of gruit. Hops, which could be grown by any small holder, were favored as Protestantism and resistance to the secular power of the Church spread across Northern Europe. Some scholars think of the Reinheitsgebot (Appendix C) as an assertion, not of beer purity but of the renunciation of church domination of the brewing trade. Others point to the provision that prices of beer could be raised by the authorities as evidence that it was intended to protect supplies of wheat for bread bakers. See the note on Tongue Mapping in chapter 1.

Beer fermenting in an open-top fermenter.

After boiling, the wort is cooled quickly by going through a heat exchanger. Yeast is added ("pitched" is the brewers' term) and fermentation begins. These days, most fermentation takes place in closed, temperature-controlled stainless steel vessels, although a few places retain the old-fashioned open vats.

It's important to note that not all the starch in malted grain is converted to sugar in mashing and that not all the carbohydrates (starch and sugar) in the wort are converted to alcohol. Producing a wort with lots of unfermentable sugars makes for a beer with a heavy body. Stopping fermentation before all the fermentable sugar is converted to alcohol leaves a beer with some sweetness.

"If beer were to be invented today . . . we would almost certainly make beer directly from barley using enzymes, we would not heat and cool and dry and wet the process as much as we do today and we would not dilute the bulk product and fill it into tiny heavy packages for distribution! The process would be a good deal more rational."

Michael Lewis and Tom W. Young, *Brewing*

Carbonation

Until recently, the carbon dioxide of fermentation was released into the atmosphere. These days, brewers of brands like Pilsner Urquell are recapturing what would otherwise be a contribution to global warming and reusing it later to add the sparkle to their beer. Speaking of bubbles, most beer today is carbonated by being stored in a closed container with an atmosphere of pressurized carbon dioxide above it. The cold beer absorbs the gas, and both together are then filtered and transferred to kegs, cans or bottles. (For what it's worth, all beer is "cold-filtered" because there's no other way to do it.) The more elegant path to fizziness is called bottle conditioning. The completely fermented beer gets an additional dose of sugars and maybe a shot of new yeast. This revitalized beer is capped up in bottles where the yeast goes to work on the sugar and creates a tiny amount of carbon dioxide gas. The gas, being trapped in the bottle with no way of escape, dissolves in the beer to make the sparkle. The yeast remains in the bottle too and in the course of aging, it breaks down and adds new complexities to the flavor of the beer. Almost all home-brewed beer is bottle-conditioned and this little flourish may be one of the reasons for homebrewing's continued and increasing popularity. What all these choices add up to is a recipe. If a wine's flavor is the product of the soil and climate where the grape is grown, a beer's flavor is the product of its recipe. Some of these recipes are pretty similar to one another, and among the cognoscenti, these families of

Conditioning tanks, where the beer is stored before it's ready to be served.

Harvesting yeast to be reused at the Philadelphia Brewing Company.

recipes and their beers are called Beer Styles.

Fermented beer usually goes through a period of conditioning before it's ready to package and drink. Conditioning vessels allow the yeast to settle out of the beer and be drawn off for reuse.

Can I Make My Own?

You bet. In fact homebrewers have some advantages over their commercial colleagues. Anyone who can make a good thick soup or a decent beef stew can make beer. There are four reasons why anyone might want to.

Freshness

There is one thing that every beer lover knows; the best beers in the world may not arrive at your home port in the best condition. We'll talk about this some more in the next chapter, but if your favorite style of beer is from far away, a lot of bottles are going to disappoint you. A lover of Scotch Ale who lives in Alaska might just have to learn to make the stuff to insure a fresh or properly matured supply.

Meditation on Beer

. The most sensitive and well-trained palate in the world will never attend to, take apart, reintegrate and rhapsodize on a flavor as thoroughly as the average palate that has built that flavor once or twice from scratch. You will have a more intimate relationship with your homemade beer than with any other foodstuff. You will examine, probe, evaluate and think about your homemade beer more intensely than most people think about anything. The intense focus will probably make you more aware of the characteristics of the other beers you drink. Even if your homebrewed beer shows up rarely on your table, it is bound to make you think about beer and to help you enjoy all the other beers you taste.

Pride in Craftsmanship

Let's face it, there's not much left that you can make at home that outshines its commercial counterparts. I can think of four things; soup, beer, pizza and love. Perhaps you have some others. It may be vitally important to you to have a real, simple, single thing that you do that doesn't need to be hyphenated to be understood. At work you may be an adjunct-manufacturing-data-systems-analyst. By the time you explain to someone what it is you do, you've forgotten it yourself. At home you can be a Daddy Lover Brewer Baker. When someone asks your five-year-old what daddy does, she can say, "He kisses mommy, bakes bread and makes beer." If you pay attention, you can say the same thing. Best of all, you can share what you do in the simplest and most direct way imaginable: "Here, have a beer."

Satisfying an Idiosyncratic Taste

The homebrewer can, with just a little practice and diligence, have exactly the beer he wants to drink. Since the homebrewer doesn't have stockholders to mollify, he can spend as much on ingredients as he wants. He can monitor the development of the beer in the cellar, notice how it matures and drink it at its best. The beginning homebrewer lets someone else do the malting and mashing for him. He buys the result, a concentrated malt extract in a can or plastic pouch. He dilutes the extract with water, adds pelletized hops and brings it to a boil. After the boil, the brewer takes steps to chill the wort. When the wort cools down, he adds yeast and sets it aside to ferment. The boiling takes about an hour. Fermentation can last for three to ten days, the time depending on the ambient temperature and the specific gravity of the wort (heat speeds up the fermentation).

When fermentation is done, he primes the beer with a small amount of sugar and puts it in squeaky-clean bottles. The sugar starts a secondary fermentation. The bottle traps the CO_2 from the fermentation and that carbonates the beer. This, by the way, is a kind of carbonation known as bottle conditioning. Some of the best beers in the world are bottle conditioned, so the home brewer has another advantage over most commercial brewers. How good is this beer? It's better than a lot of what you can buy. Some beer, the English ale known as "bitter" for example, can be replicated nicely with this simple process. These concentrates, which used to be made primarily for the baking industry, are being more finely tuned for the homebrewer all the time. You can tinker with the kits, adding this and that to change the flavor just as you might add your own seasonings to canned spaghetti sauce. There are even some deluxe malt extract kits. If you like the styles of beer they offer, these kits can give you first-class results with just a bit of doctoring.

It's just a little bit more trouble to buy and steep your own grains, extracting the sugar and then boiling it. This adds two or three hours to the process. Because the sugar doesn't undergo a long cooking to concentrate it for canning, the beer is livelier tasting. You can even make a credible imitation of many of the world's beer styles. The best way to get started is to talk to an expert brewer. Track one down at a homebrew supply store or club. See the bibliography for books with more complete instructions and recipes. Maybe you've tasted homemade wine, and maybe it wasn't as good as even inexpensive commercial wine. The problem there is that you need good grapes to make good wine, and good grapes are in short supply. They never end up in those cans or buckets that get shipped to home wine makers.

Beer, on the other hand, is made from common ingredients that are widely available. You can even grow a usable portion of yeast from a small sample obtained from certain beer bottles. The best beers in the world spring from good brewers using simple stuff according to a great recipe.

Getting Help

If this seems daunting, there is tutoring available. There are 1200 homebrew supply shops in the United States according to the Home Wine and Beer Trade Association. Homebrewing is a wonderfully folksy pastime, and the people who like it enough to open stores that sell homebrew supplies tend to be friendly and informative. Most of them sell kits that contain everything you need to brew your first batch and a generous stream of advice (and ingredients) for brewing your next couple hundred.

If that seems a bit intimidating, you might check around for a U-brew shop. These are combined shops and mini-breweries that provide brewing assistance. In Canada, where high taxes make beer about twice as expensive as it is in the US, many beer lovers are making the switch to brewing their own. Instead of tackling the challenge of small-scale brewing by themselves, they head down to the local U-brew. A U-brew is a store where customers can pick out a recipe or design their own. Then they buy malt syrup, hops and yeast and rent a kettle space to boil the whole thing up. After the wort has cooled, it goes into a container with some yeast and stays at the shop to ferment. After a couple of weeks the customers come back and bottle the stuff and take it home. Beer made this way costs about as much as the pre-tax, store-bought product.

The whole thing sounds almost unbearably quaint, but these little stores now produce 3 percent of the beer produced in the province of Ontario. In the beer business, 3 percent is a big piece of the market, and a mega-brewers lobbying group was worried enough to persuade the province to tax U-brew beer. Contrary to everybody's expectations, the tax hasn't strangled these little community breweries. People who set out to save a Canadian dollar or two are finding that they like the taste of their own individual beer. Apparently, some homebrewers are turning to U-brews for their pleasant, pub-like atmosphere and for the pleasure of leaving the cleaning up to someone else.

Homebrewer fermentation lock: gas rising from the beer bubbles out through the water-filled tube. Air cannot come in contact with the beer.

A Gateway to Brewing

Cider making provides an even simpler introduction to brewing. Cider is a delicious and refreshing drink made by fermenting apple juice. It is not beer, but I include it here for four reasons. First, it has a fresh and aromatic immediacy that appeals to most beer drinkers. Second, it's a very easy drink to make yourself and is often a transitional first step into homebrewing. Third, it was, for colonial Americans, a substitute for ale in the days when barley malt was scarce. Finally, most of us have never tasted a really good glass of cider and it's hard to resist the opportunity to point out something delicious.

Homebrewer equipment: everything you need to brew except for one big pot.

You can make cider from a glass or plastic gallon of juice just by replacing the bottle cap with a fermentation lock in a one-hole stopper (See photo opposite.) and letting nature take its course.

You get the best results if the cider is very tart. Some people will want to add a cup to a pound of brown sugar to each gallon of juice to increase both the alcohol and the stability of the cider. A bit of citric acid or the juice of a lemon isn't a bad touch either. After a day or two fermenting on the countertop, the cider should be placed in the refrigerator, loosely capped. Let me repeat that last: loosely capped. That means with the cap just barely resting on top of the cider jug.

If you want sparkling cider, follow the procedures for bottle-conditioning beer given below.

Even better results can be had by fermenting the apple juice with a deliberately introduced yeast. Delicate apple flavors are preserved with champagne yeast; a Belgian or English ale yeast makes for a heartier product. Some homebrewers salvage an ounce or two of yeast after their batch of beer is done and use it to make a bonus jug of cider. Bakers yeast will give you (surprise!) a bakeshop aroma that's pleasant. You can spice it up with cloves or a cinnamon stick, but this somehow seems to miss the spirit of the thing. Of course, you'll have to pick apple juice that has no preservatives—like potassium metabisulfate—added. Fermentation is exactly what the preservatives were added to prevent. If apples aren't your favorite fruit, you can ferment any juice that doesn't have preservatives. Look for juices whose nutrition label announces at least 30gm of carbohydrate for 240 ml (8 ounce) portion. Fully fermented, that will give you a cider with 6% alcohol, although you may find the drink more palatable if you stop the fermentation before all the sugar is converted.

The Next Step

Making beer is nothing more than an elaboration of the steps involved in making cider. There's a bit of equipment involved and the chances are that you already own most of it. Along with a large pot for boiling, you'll need some plastic tubing, a thermometer, a gauge for measuring the density of the wort and a few cases of bottles to get started. See your local homebrew supply shop for ingredients and instructions.

The Social Brewer

We're North Americans so we join clubs. American people who brew small amounts of beer for themselves and their friends join homebrew clubs. These clubs do a lot to promote more and better beer. They also have some wonderful and unrepentantly sophomoric names, a few of which I pass along to you here:

The San Andreas Malts

The Maltose Falcons

Homebrewers of Philadelphia and the Suburbs (HOPS)

Brewers United for Real Pilsner (BURP)

New Jersey Worthogs

The Draught Board

If the puns here aren't obvious to you or if you can't get enough of them, go to this website for even more:

http://www.shortcourseinbeer.com

The Scene

This business of enjoying locally brewed craft beers and maybe even making your own and sharing it with friends has engendered a social scene. Just as clubs based on hunting or motorcycle riding or yacht ownership generate a style of interaction, brewing clubs seem to have their own atmosphere, a relaxed, flannel shirt sort of ambience, with a lot of food loving and home gardening thrown in. Male competition frenzy is at a minimum and there is a significant female minority. It's possible that beer brewing itself will become an important pastime for a lot of people just because of the pleasure of hanging out with other brewers.

For up-to-date information on homebrewing, go to:

http://www.beertown.org/homebrewing/index.html or

http://www.homesweethomebrew.com/

To learn more about the brewing industry in America, visit:

http://www.beerinstitute.org

Discussion Questions

1. Do you still want to quit your job and go to work in the brewery?

2. What's stopping you from running out and getting a gallon of cider?

3. What do you imagine fermented orange juice would taste like? What about mango, pineapple or pomegranate? If you fermented grape juice, do you think it would taste like the wine you're used to?
4. If you could brew the beer of your dreams, what would it taste like?

Chapter 5

Enjoying Beer

When you have read to the end of this chapter you will
• have enough knowledge to pass as a beer maven
• enjoy your next glass of beer a little bit more than you did your last one

Between mere guzzling and a mature connoisseurship, there is a small but measurable gap. A bit of knowledge is the difference. Most beer in America is gulped, not tasted. If you would like to join the happy minority and enjoy some of the best imports as well as the new offerings from large and small craft brewers, here are some considerations.

Freshness

Beer deteriorates after it has been bottled, and freshly bottled beer tastes as good as it ever will. (There are a few bottle-conditioned exceptions: see the entries under barley wine, abbey beers and Trappist ales.) If you've ever been disappointed with an exotic imported beer, there's a good chance that it had been aged or stored in a way that accelerated its deterioration.

The best way to insure fresh beer in a tavern or restaurant is to order a beer that's brewed on the premises. The next best strategy is to ask your server what beers are fresh or which ones sell a lot. He or she will usually give you a straight answer. Your question implies that you know your beer and a tip could hang in the balance.

It's also helpful to read label marks. Some few enlightened breweries put either the bottling date or the "pull date" explicitly on the bottle. The pull date represents the last day that the beer should be on sale.

Freshness isn't exactly a hot topic among most beer consumers; market research done by Pittsburgh Brewing Company indicates that consumers are not particularly aware that fresh beer tastes better. Many industry observers thought that Anheuser-Busch was misguided when it introduced the born-on date.

Many breweries notch their labels or imprint their twenty-four-bottle cases with a code that indicates the date of bottling. This enables the distributor to know the bottling or pull date, but conceals it from the public. If you know the code, you know the age of the beer. Beer that's kept cold will have a longer shelf life than beer that's stored at room temperature.

A common dating method is called the Julian Code. Look for four or five numbers. The first three are the day of the year: 123 means the 123rd day of the year (the 2nd or 3rd of May) and the last number(s) indicate the year. So 1231 tells you that the beer was bottled early in May 2011.

Temperature

Most beer is served too cold to be tasted. As a rule, darker, richer beers and complex ales should be served at higher temperatures (50° to 55°F) than pale, crisp lagers, which are best around 45°F. Good bars will store and serve beer at the appropriate temperature and they will never offer you beer in a frozen glass. When a beer advertisement urges you to have a "frosty cold mug" of something or other, just what are they trying to hide?

Context

Just as with wine, the taste of beer changes the taste of your food. In turn the beer is affected by the food. If you find a beer to be too powerfully flavored, try it with food. If it's still too strong, try it with more powerfully flavored food. There are beer and food combinations that are as traditional as wine and food pairings. Salmon and pilsner, oysters and stout are rightly celebrated in Europe and hoppy beer is especially right with the spicy foods of Mexico, India, Thailand and Szechuan.

One attempt to simplify the relationship between food and drink is the sentiment "What grows together, goes together." The attractive prejudice behind that notion is that farmers, vintners and brewers have somehow choreographed perfect harmonies over centuries of practice, but the idea is more romantic than real. The truth is that local food and drink combinations tend to become better over time, but it's often possible to do much better when you combine tastes from different regions.

Try Belgian tripel with mole poblano, Witbier with guacamole, a Bohemian Pilsner with Korean Soon Doo Boo or IPA with fried peppers and pasta.

Glasses.

Beer glasses should be clean and very well rinsed. In Belgium, where they make a study of these things, many beers have their own specially sized and shaped glass. Frozen glasses chill your lips and numb your taste; they are best reserved for beer that doesn't taste very good.

"Did you ever taste beer?"
"I had a sip of it once," said the small servant.
"Here's a state of things!" cried Mr. Swiveller ... "She never tasted it—it can't be tasted in a sip!"
—Charles Dickens

The question seems to be: how do you maximize the experience

One style of Pilsner glass with unusually bulbous bottom, at the Budvar brewery in the Czech Republic..

The characteristic chalice-like Chimay glass.

of aroma coming off a cool beverage. At first blush, it might seem like an exaggerated fishbowl shape would do the trick: lots of evaporative surface and then a narrow opening to concentrate the aromas rising off the surface. In fact, a lot of purpose-built beer glasses take this approach. Some even add a bit of chimney.

My experience, based on exhaustive comparative tasting, is that the most revealing glass—the one that exposes more of the luscious smells of beer—is also the ideal wine glass, or a larger version of it. It's a stemmed glass with a bowl around the dimensions of an index card: 3 x 5 to 3.5 x 5.5 inches/75 x 125mm. The smaller end of the range is represented by Riedel's Ouverture Red Wine glass, which at this writing can be had for about 8USD a stem.

For most of beer's history it was a cloudy drink with not much to see and glass was a great luxury. Beer in the ancient world was drunk from pots and through straws with strainers that filtered out the heavy stuff. Argentinean *maté* drinkers use a similar arrangement today. Pottery containers, of which steins are the most exuberant

The thistle-shaped Duvel glass.

example, have probably held most of the world's beer. The English tankard is an oversized metal or wooden cup with a handle. In England, a leather container coated with pitch or tar called a blackjack was also used.

There are four attributes of a beer glass that have come to be prized.

Cleanliness To be "beer-clean," a beer glass should be free of grease, soap and detergent film. These substances destroy the head on a glass of beer and sometimes leave their own flavor to boot.

Some glass-cleaning systems leave an unpleasant chlorine odor in the glass and should be avoided unless you enjoy a beer at the pool so much that you like to have a little of the pool in your beer.

The simplest way to make your glasses beer-clean is to use an alkaline dishwashing detergent and a very thorough rinse. It's also a good idea to give empty glasses an occasional sniff to make sure you get a good clean whiff of nothing at all. Any genuine beer-oriented bar or brewpub will have given this matter some serious thought and should be happy to tell you all about their own procedures.

Clarity Part of the pleasure of beer is the contemplation of the color; clear to cloudy, light to dark. Tinted or opaque glasses should be saved for milk.

Smoothness Roughness on the inside of a glass provides sites for bubbles to form. A glass with a lot of interior roughness encourages gushing and an overlarge head. An extreme example of this is the Styrofoam cup used for coffee-to-go. Pour some beer in one to get an idea of the effect of rough spots in a beer glass. Beer glasses that become scratched should be demoted to other use, and disposable beer cups should be clear plastic.

Tradition Certain beer styles have particularly shaped glasses associated with them. Some folks consider this over-delicate frippery; others consider it an additional dimension to their pleasure. In either event, let's avoid beer snobbery.

Pictured opposite are a few traditional shapes.

Specialty glassware at Monk's Cafe in Philadelphia.

Aside from these formal considerations, there are a few other things that you should know about in order to better taste your beer.

Community

Good, delicious, honestly made beer seems to inspire community these days. Maybe it's the sense of taking a stand for quality in the midst of a world that seems to care only for mass marketing. Maybe it's the vaguely counter-cultural tone to all this cereal and herbal stuff. Or maybe it's just the alcohol.

Whatever's behind it, you can see beer communities emerging. Some of them are the informal groups of patrons at the growing numbers of craft-oriented bars. Others are the more formal, if not necessarily more intimate groups, like the homebrewers mentioned earlier and the growing number of online communities.

And yes, community does make beer taste better. It works like this: if you're hosting a tasting or even just posting your own tasting notes, you pay attention to your sensations and you allow your impressions to be expanded by listening to other people's. Beer makes other people more pleasant and vice versa.

For a partial list of community resources, go to
http://www.shortcourseinbeer.com/resources

Beer with Flavor

You can't assume that every beer on offer in a bar actually has a taste. It used to be that if you wanted to hear about the good stuff, you asked the bartender what imports she had. Recently, American beers have gotten better and the best-selling imported beers are more likely to be impeccable but dull. You can't ask for "the good stuff"; that's too snooty and probably won't get you the information that you're looking for. How do you enquire after the beers you want to choose from in as polite and efficient a way as possible?

One thing that seems to work is "got any beer with flavor?" Most barkeeps know what you mean and no one seems to take offence. If you're too shy for even that, you can ask for the freshest beer in the house. That may not be exactly what you want, but it gets you right in to the interesting end of the ballpark.

Bouquet

The combination of smells that a particular beer offers. Bouquet in beers that are served chilled is more subtle than in wines. It only takes a little experience to learn to distinguish the aroma of hops, which is usually sharp and herbal, from the smell of malt, which can be sweet and earthy. A bit more practice and you'll be able to distinguish the citrusy American hop varieties from their more herbal European cousins.

Beer Engine

This is a traditional English hand pump for drawing unpressurized cask or real ale from the cellar of a pub. If you find yourself in a place where the bartender is pumping lightly carbonated real ale from the cellar with vigorous strokes of the beer engine, you're in the company of serious beer drinkers indeed. The beers are often matured in the keg and referred to as "cask conditioned."

Real Ale is the term that preservationists in the UK use to describe their traditional cask-conditioned ales. The implication is that the industrially produced, blander ales and lagers that are displacing Real Ale are imposters.

Bitterness

The amount of bitterness in any particular beer is measured chemically and expressed in Bitterness Units (BUs). Commercially available beers are almost all in the range of 15 to 20 BUs, and a malt beverage has to have at least 11 BUs to be called "beer" in the United States. Some beer styles depend more heavily on bitterness than others. Belgian Witbier, for instance, is made with 20 BUs, while India Pale Ale will have 40 BUs or more. Since bitterness has to be in proportion to other flavors, beers that have little malt character usually have the minimum amount of bitterness.

Homebrewers, who have to add bitterness to their recipes, use units that describe the bittering potential of particular varieties of hops. These measures multiply the percentage of the weight of the hops that is made of the bitter alpha acid by the total weight of the hops and are given as AAUs (alpha acid units) or HBUs (homebrewers' bitterness units).

Body

Body is the sensation of weight or thickness that a beer has in the mouth. The difference between a full-bodied and a light-bodied beer is like the difference between skim and whole milk. Light-bodied beers taste more bubbly than full-bodied ones. A lot of our experience of a beer's richness is dependent on this mouth feeling. Body in wine is mostly the effect of glycerine, a product of fermentation. In beer it is largely attributable to dextrins, which are unfermented sugars, and to proteins from the grain.

Finish

Finish is the sensation that a beer leaves behind in your mouth after it is swallowed. It's a matter of both flavor and aroma. Most drinks leave an aftertaste of one sort or another, but a lot of the charm of beer is in the finish, and many of the truly astounding beers in this world get their effect from their long, haunting finishes. The really great finishes stun you and make you want to take another taste. Finish may be a large part of what makes some people fall in love with particular beers.

I asked a beer-oriented chef from San Francisco about the matter. Here's what he wrote:

> We're at the Toronado over on Haight St., and I turned my friend on to the best beer in the world . . . the one laced with pink elephants. I coached him a little and he discovered nutmeg, clove, and honey aromas. I asked him about the fruit (I get screaming bananas with Delerium*). He said he tasted some, but he didn't sound convinced. Then after we finished our beers he said, "Holy shit, I just breathed in and it felt like I huffed some banana gas."
>
> So is this "complexity"? Is it that sensation that even though you're finished drinking, you're getting allusions to banana or sour apple or pie spice whisping across your palate? This happens for people like us regularly, but do you remember the first time it happened to you? I don't exactly, but I remember the feeling, it was the sort of thing that inspires people to want to learn more about beer.

Francis Hogan

*(He's talking about Delerium Tremens from Belgium)

The best way to become an expert on finishes is to pay attention. Just notice the sensation that any drink leaves in your mouth. Do it with everything you taste, or at least do it as often as you remember. Two or three days of serious attention and you're on to something. A week and you're a connoisseur.

By the way, "Dry beer" is made without the flavor components that give beer a finish, just as "Light beer" is made without attention to the components that give it body.

Fruity

As an adjective describing the taste of beer, fruity refers to compounds called esters that are formed during fermentation, not to any fruit that was involved in the beer making. The qualities of ale recall the characteristics of fruit, and fruits get some of their flavor from esters of their own. Our language being somewhat short on words describing flavor, and estery not being something that your mother talked about when she made mashed bananas, we may have to make do with fruity as a description for a while.

Head

Head is the common name for the wonderful crown of foam that appears on a freshly poured glass of beer. It's one of the devices by which a cool or cold glass of beer manages to deliver a full measure of aroma (the other is carbonation). Like every other foam, the head on a glass of beer is made up of bubbles; thin films of liquid surrounding pockets of gas. The gas in a head of beer comes from carbon dioxide that's released from solution when a beer is opened or poured.

Foams in pure liquids are very short-lived. Water bubbling out of the tap goes flat in seconds, its bubbles collapsing in response to two forces. First, the water in the film is pulled down by gravity, destroying the film as it goes. Second, all liquids exhibit a characteristic called surface tension, a mild mutual attraction between molecules of the liquid. Molecules on the surface of a liquid are much fonder of each other than they are of the air and so tend to collapse back into the embrace of their fellows. The walls of bubbles in a foam are only a few molecules thick so gravity and surface tension tend to pull them apart quickly.

The foam on a head of beer lasts as long as it does because beer has ingredients that combat these two forces. Huge molecules like dextrins—which also contribute to the body of the beer—make the beer thicker and slow down the rate of flow. A particular large protein from the grain itself and some acids from the hops help to reduce surface tension.

As anyone who has ever beaten egg whites to a foam can tell you, fats are the enemies of froth. Barley malt contains between 1 and 2 percent lipids, but most of these are destroyed in brewing. The most likely sources of head-reducing fats are your glass and your lips. Glasses that are not beer-clean and plastic containers in general can retain a layer of fatty material. A drinker's lips can be greased with cosmetic and medicinal greases, lipsticks and lip balms. Grease can also come from recently eaten food, and in fact many common bar snacks are so fatty that they could be burned for illumination if the power fails.

Cooking with Beer

Wine and beer both have tremendous power to change and often to elevate some pretty ordinary food. It's worth noting that most cooking methods boil off most of the alcohol in beer. Cooking also changes the flavors drastically, destroying any subtle flavors and magnifying a few obvious ones. That's why we don't waste great wine or beer by cooking with it. It's also why bad wine or beer should be poured in the sink, not in the pan.

Beer is a good base liquid for steaming mussels or clams provided that herbs are used that round out the native bitterness or that relatively unhopped beers go in the pot.

Beer is also useful to deglaze a pan, that is, to dissolve the brownings on the bottom of a sauté pan in an added liquid. Beer is often used, either alone or in a mixture with broth, as a deglazer. Sometimes the resulting liquid is reduced by cooking and evaporation to make a sauce; this is called a reduction. The deglazing liquid or reduction can be thickened with cream or roux or starch to make a simple sauce.

Cooks should note that concentrating the beer also concentrates the bitterness at the same time that it destroys aroma. It's probably best to begin your experiments by using just enough liquid to dissolve the pan brownings or again to pick a malty, rather than a hoppy beer.

Mixed Drinks

I don't know a single person who drinks them, but there are a surprising number of traditional drinks involving beer and something else. The few that I've tried actually highlight some characteristic of beer by putting it in a strange context: see Shandy and Buttered Ale. The most celebrated mixed drink is wassail. Mixed beer drinks may prove to be a whole new frontier for those who enjoy being out ahead of everybody.

Black and tan is originally Guinness stout and light lager: by extension, any mixture of a dark and a light beer to produce an intermediate.

A **boilermaker** is a shot of whisky poured into a glass of beer. The effect intended is not an enhancement of hoppy or malty flavors.

A **depth charge** is a boilermaker's crude cousin. The shot glass of whisky is dropped into the beer and the entire thing consumed.

Despite what you may think, there is little dental damage caused by the shot glass sliding into the drinker's mouth because most people who drink depth charges already have no teeth.

Nuts-and-bolts, a mixture of mild and bitter.

Buttered ale is sugar, cinnamon, butter and hot ale.

Shandy is beer and ginger ale; lemon shandy is beer and lemon soda.

Calichal is a Mexican idea, one part beer, four parts pulque.

Kindel Berliner Weisse is a north German wheat beer served kir-like with raspberry syrup.

Pouring

The perfect glass of your favorite beer has a head that's about an inch (25mm) high. In America, it's sometimes called a nickel head after the diameter of our five-cent coin. That's about enough to give you a taste of the foam, not so much that you can't get some beer when you tilt the glass for your first sip. To get the perfect glass, start with a beer-clean glass and beer at the right temperature. The glass should be at room temperature, not chilled or frozen.

Tilt the glass at a forty-five-degree angle and pour the beer gently down the side. There should be little or no foam. When the glass is three-fourths full, turn it upright and continue pouring straight down the center, creating a head.

This careful pouring is a success when it helps you shut out distractions and focus on what you're about to taste. It's a failure if you cave in to obsessive behavior and try for the perfect nickel.

Sipping Insipid?

For all this talk of tastes and tasting, we still have to admit that there are a lot of people who don't like flavor at all and who particularly don't like the flavor of malt and hops and yeast. That's right, there are lots of grown-ups who don't like the taste of beer. However, many of them would enjoy taking part in the sociability of beer drinking. For those people, there's a world of beers having little or no flavor. The style is called CAP or Common American Pilsner. It's sometimes also called Lawnmower Beer. The insipidity of these beers can be enhanced by chilling them to near their freezing point and serving them with lots of distractions.

You can tell which beers are most likely to be in this category by looking at their advertising. If the featured beer is shown as a part of frenzied sociability or the background to some serious flirting or the cool-off after some intense physical activity, chances are great that the beer has little or no taste.

For a current list of low-flavor beers determined by our tasting panel, consult **http://www.shortcourseinbeer.com/insipid**

Serving Temperatures

Isn't it just like some smartass beer writer to tell you that the proper serving temperature for Dem Ouden Frucktbier is 62° to 63°F? Don't you just love it when he tells you about the great beers he tasted when he visited the fourteenth century Oberscupper brewery high in the Bavarian Alps? Next thing you know, the sonafabitch will be advocating thistle-shaped glasses with gold-plated rims and tinted light bulbs to accentuate the color.

Just how, short of a separate beer refrigerator, are you supposed to get your special beers to their very special temperatures? Here's a rough guideline based on the fact that the bottom shelf of most home refrigerators will keep liquids stored at something like 38—40°F/3—4°C. Let your Heineken, Miller and similar pils sit on the kitchen counter for ten minutes before you flip the cap. Darker beers and ones with pronounced maltiness can sit out for longer—up to thirty minutes for a barley wine. A soak in water straight from the tap will accelerate the process.

In any case, don't make this into a fetish and don't be intimidated by beer snobs. We don't want to hear about thirsty people pacing back and forth with a stopwatch in hand while their beer warms up.

Sometimes the best place for beer to warm up is in your mouth.

Thanks to a growing number of wine lovers who want to keep their favorite drink from harm while they're waiting to pull the cork, almost every home warehouse-type store in the country carries small, inexpensive refrigerators that allow some control over temperature. Depending on your particular beer collection, you can probably find one that keeps your beer right where you want it.

Soapy Flavors

These show up in beer from time to time. They may be the product of badly prepared glasses. These flavors can also be the result of the normal action of certain strains of yeast that produce a series of acids (hexanoic, octanoic, etc.) that resemble soap. These acids are present in all beers to some extent. Excess of soapy flavor usually happens at higher gravities and some yeast strains produce more than others.

Variability

You fall in love with a beer at a bar in Miami. Next week, over lunch in Philadelphia, you order it and you feel the little rush of anticipation: *this is going to be great.* Maybe you even talk your companions into giving it a try. This is, you assure them, the best thing in beer since they started putting the head on the top instead of the bottom. When the beer arrives, it's disappointing, flat, dull and tasteless.

What happened?

Here are some of the possibilities. In all but giant industrial breweries, each batch of beer is going to be very slightly different from the next. Barley is an agricultural product and this year's crop is bound to be just slightly different from last year's. Hops vary too, and so does municipal water and even brewers themselves.

You could be different too. Your palate changes its sensitivity depending on the time of day, the state of your health and what you just ate. There may be dozens of other factors involved, each with its own little research grant waiting to support its investigation.

But these are the sources of small differences, ones that arouse your curiosity. They are certainly not powerful enough to lead to outright disappointment. Things that make good beer taste bad are age, bad storage and contaminated glasses. Bad storage includes freezing as well as overheating.

Practical cures for variability include buying from a place that sells a lot of your beer, buying from a place that handles its beer carefully (and passes the cost on to you) and buying beers that are local and therefore less exposed to the slings and arrows of outrageous importation. "Close to the source" could become the fashionable description of the right way to get beer. Brewpubs and home-brewing are the obvious answers and both are growing rapidly.

As more consumers become aware of the role the wholesaler and the barman play, you can expect to see more advertising directed to concerns about freshness and local origin. Ultimately, the superiority of freshly made, well-handled beer may, in some markets, diminish the snob appeal of imported labels.

Food and Wine, Food and Beer

Probably nothing discomfits diners aspiring to sophistication as much as the problem of choosing a beverage to go with their meal. It's time to get over it. The whole notion of "rightness" comes from the wine-drinking world as it existed until a few years ago, where knowledge of the proper was a measure of social standing and gentle upbringing. Real wine lovers have left that tense, judgmental attitude behind a long time ago. There's no point at all in transporting it to beer.

Beer and wine are different companions for food, however. The main difference is that while both drinks refresh the mouth, they use different mechanisms. The main impressions of beer are bitterness, spice, malt and carbonation. Table wines impress us with fruit, acid, sweetness and tannin as their main characteristics. We tend to drink greater quantities of beer and to enjoy it at cooler temperatures than red wine and at warmer temperatures than white. The taste of wine changes in the company of salty or sweet dishes and can be really abused by some others like artichokes or asparagus. Beer is sturdier, keeping its own taste and having more of an effect on the taste of the food than wine would.

Fortunately it is possible to navigate your way brilliantly through a beer list at dinner even if you are unfamiliar with any of the beers on it. There are two important principles involved in pairing beer successfully with food.

The first principle is that it's hard to make a bad match. Go ahead, try it. At least in terms of entrees (main dishes) there are very few good beers that don't provide a pleasant accompaniment to good food. This is so in part because "with" food is really a misnomer. We really drink beer or wine between bites of food so the effect of one on the other is not so dramatic. Another reason that it's hard to make a bad match is that we are capable of enjoying contrasting flavors as well as complementary ones. Occasionally a beer will be so bitter as to poison the taste of a food or so mild as to be lost beside it, but, aside from industrial beers, these instances are rare.

Incidentally, I recommend that you try finding bad matches of food to beer. The most common result of the search is to find new and surprising great combinations. The few really awful combinations that you might come up with have their purpose too: they can shock your taste buds into a heightened understanding of both the food and the beer. Maybe you might want to take a perfectly respectable beer like Anchor Porter or Sierra Nevada Pale Ale and try to find food that doesn't work with them. Go for three combinations for each one (main courses only, no desserts). Try them. You may

find something truly awful, but I'll bet that if you keep an open mind you'll find some purposefully bad combination that's really good.

Deliberately looking for the worst is sometimes a powerful creative tool. Think of it as the Mel Brooks rule. Do you remember his movie, *The Producers*? Two con men sell shares in a Broadway musical. Since they have more investment money than the play costs to produce, they want the show to flop: then they can pocket the oversubscribed money. So they create what they think is the worst show possible; a musical called *Springtime for Hitler* that has production numbers featuring dancing Nazis. They try so hard to make it bad that it turns out to be an outrageous spoof that everybody loves.

There's a law of the universe at work here.

The second principle is, match weight instead of flavors. Full-bodied beers tend to go well with robust foods, light beers with more delicate ones.

Very spicy dishes tend to overwhelm the flavor of any beverage. If you are ordering attack cuisine—Thai, Szechuan or their spiritual cousins—pick a beer that has either pronounced sweetness or bitterness. These two characteristics will come through in spite of megadoses of hot pepper.

All that said, there are still certain combinations that have come to be thought of as classics. I urge them on you with all the vigor of a movie buff dragging you off to see *Citizen Kane*.

Guinness Stout and oysters. The bitterness of the stout is perfect with the salty, taste-of-the-ocean tang of the oyster.

Belhaven Scottish Ale (or one of its stronger cousins: see Scotch Ale) and mincemeat pie.

Hoppy American lager with barbecue.

Almost any wheat beer with grilled fish.

Duvel and sweet barbecue, Chimay or Allagash Tripel with the North Carolina style.

Juicy fat grilled salmon with pilsner

Framboise and a ripe peach

For some refined suggestions, check out Garrett Oliver's *The Brewmaster's Table*.

Discussion Questions
1. Is it possible that the deliberate search for bad combinations could lead you to some really great discoveries? How might that work? What combinations are you sure would be awful? Are you really sure?
2. From the website http://www.shortcourseinbeer.com click on the beer recipes. If there's one you'd like to try, imagine what the beer would contribute to the dish.
3. Does all this talk about glasses and serving temperature seem silly? Why not assemble a few different glasses and try one beer in several? Are there differences? Can you smell things in one glass that are "invisible" in another?

Chapter 6

A Dictionary of Beer Talk

When you finish this chapter you will

- understand most of what's being said in any beer conversation
- be aware of some of the complexity behind what you're tasting
- be able to take part in the fun

There's a lot to this beer world: a recent online poll dredged up 76,000 beers produced by 8000 breweries. First, let's simplify things by dealing with the three most important beer words: beer, ale and lager.

What Is Beer ?

I'll follow the crowd in saying that the word "beer" usually refers to a fermented drink made from grain and flavored with hops. Labeling laws in the US extend the definition by requiring anything called beer to have minimum amounts of alcohol and to conform to traditional understandings of what beer is. The law and current usage make exception for those very few drinks, like Belgian wheat beer, groot, spruce beer and Finnish sahti that rely on some seasoning other than hops.

In recognition of spiritual kinship, but not commercial competition, the word beer is extended to those preindustrial drinks made from grain using low-tech mashing.

Deliberately excluded from this definition are carbonated drinks that make no reference to either malt or hops in their flavor but may be sold through traditional beer outlets. They have names like alcopop and malternative, and they're designed for a market that isn't sufficiently grown up for the taste of beer, but wants a dosage of alcohol in about the same strength and in a similar container. Alco-pops and malternatives may be alcoholic, but they aren't beer.

We'll divide the beer world into two parts: Ales and Lagers.

What Is Ale?

Descriptive beer words are not, like the other descriptors that make modern life possible, completely definable. A definition, after all, is a way of making something finite or finished. Not a bad thing, this: it enables us to get bread flour when we need to bake bread and type O positive when we need to transfuse. Hooray for definition.

Beers and beer styles, on the other hand, resist definition. They foam up out of their boundaries and run down the sides of their limitations. They release a lot of bouquet and flavor in the process, so let's not complain. Beer words are cultural artifacts with sticky little histories that follow them around, each meaning clinging to the word even as new meanings are added. To know what ale means, we have to act like anthropologists and patiently collect all the usages and see what they add up to. The reward of this kind of work is not a definition you can consult to determine if something fits or doesn't. The reward is appreciation and a sense of initiation into a mystery. Hooray again.

At the time of the Norman Conquest of England, Danish speak-ers called a fermented grain drink *ale*. Anglo-Saxons called it *beer*. The word beer eventually dropped out of use and the word ale be-came the original English name for a drink fermented from brewed grain.

Sometime in the 1500s, English trade with the Flemish intro-duced an ale flavored with hops. This ale came to be known in Eng-lish as beer, and the distinction between beer and ale then became the presence or absence of hops. Within a century, most British beers were hopped, and unhopped ale had virtually disappeared. But the word ale had more of a following than the thing itself and it gradu-ally came to be attached to a darker, more robust product that was fermented quickly and consumed immediately at room temperature. Ale was now a hopped beverage, with the hops contributing bitterness and longevity. Beer, on the other hand, was fermented in cool places and allowed to mature for a while before being drunk. It was noticed that the yeasts that produced ales usually formed a cap on the top of the fermenting tank, while beer yeasts sank to the bottom. (Knowledge of the existence of yeast and its role in fermentation didn't exist until 1879 when Pasteur published his *Physiological Theory of Fermentation*.)

British alesters ultimately found out that a brief period of storage (or lagering) improved the quality of their ale and so adopted the technique and once again the distinction disappeared. The word ale remained to distinguish heavily flavored drinks from subtler ones.

Today, when an English drinker speaks of beer he means bitter, a top-fermented ale. The other, lighter stuff he calls lager. Americans are thinking about those bottom-fermented lagers when they ask for beer. If they want bitter, they'll call for ale.

In 1883, Emil Hansen, working at the Carlsberg brewery in Copenhagen, established that one particular variety of a single yeast species (Saccharomyces cervisiae) produced beer and that another variety produced ales. Until recently, these varieties have been distinguished by the fact that ale yeasts are warm-working top fermenters, and lager yeasts are cold-working bottom fermenters.

AHA! At last, here's a distinction you can see under a microscope. One yeast looks like this and another looks like that; one rises, one sinks; this one makes ale and this one makes beer. Sounds like a definition, doesn't it?

No, not quite. Selective breeding of yeasts is going on all the time and strains are constantly being developed that mimic some property or other of the other variety, lager yeasts that give ale accents to the flavor of the beer for instance. In our era, the distinction between the two drinks is back to a matter of esthetics. Ales have complicated, fruity aromas that come from the action of yeasts.

They tend to remind wine drinkers of some of the character of wine. Lagers are cleaner tasting and more likely to recall the flavor of malt and rely on the aroma of hops for their impact.

To make things a bit more complicated, there is no legal definition of ale in the US. Another layer of confusion comes from the state legislatures that forbid the use of the term beer when the alcohol content rises above 5 percent. In those states, ale means something that can't be called beer, regardless of how it's produced or what it tastes like. The connotation of a heartier, more alcoholic and more manly brew was briefly reinforced by the advertisers.

Who is the Ale Man?
He could be you.
The man with the thirst for
The manlier brew.
—Ballantine Ale jingle

Recently, as lager beers have taken up the inexpensive, industrial end of the beer market, ale has become the upscale drink and ordering an ale suggests, in some circles, a degree of sophistication.

Remember that ale is the name of a family of styles and also the name of a residual category of a whole bunch of brews that are made with ale yeast.

What Is Lager?

The word comes from the German *lagern*, meaning to store or lay down. It is used to describe one of the two large families of beer styles, the other being ale. The technique of lagering is apparently a medieval invention that became widely used in Germany. Beer was brewed and stored in naturally cool places like caves and cellars. During the summer months when brewing was chancy, beer was drawn from these cold reserves.

Beer that was lagered tasted different from other beer. The long storage period allowed it to drop most of its haze-making particles so the beer was clear. The yeast that developed to survive and prosper in the cold was different too. Instead of adding its own distinctive flavor notes to the beer, it left nothing at all; the beer tasted of hops, malt and the local water.

Lager first appears in America in 1840. That was when the new lagering technique and the yeast that accompanied it was introduced in the Philadelphia neighborhood of Northern Liberties by Bavarian immigrant John Wagner.

Some beer books make it seem that lager beer competed with ale and ultimately supplanted ale as the all-American drink. That's not quite true. Ale was in decline by the 1820s. The westward expansion of the new nation into Kentucky and Ohio opened up vast new farmlands and created a surplus of corn.

Before the Erie Canal opened up channels of commerce and drastically reduced the cost of transportation, it was too expensive to ship bulk corn back east. High-proof whisky, on the other hand, was concentrated, non-perishable corn. So much of it was shipped that by the mid 1820s, whisky was cheaper than milk in the big cities of the east.

Whisky killed off ale; lager came along as a Temperance drink and gradually supplanted whisky.

Not coincidentally, a wave of German immigration also began in the 1840s. The Germans established small-scale brewing operations to serve their own communities, much in the way that they established German-language newspapers and social halls.

The lagering technique was wonderfully suited to mass production and quickly supplanted ale brewing. The new-fangled beer was more congenial to hot summers and much cheaper than cloudy, pungent ales. The high carbonation levels were refreshing. It's worth remembering that ale, as we know it, was not the drink that lager supplanted. Cheap sparkling beer competed with crude homebrews (Thomas Jefferson's was an exception) made from corn and fruits and with raw locally made whiskies. Since the whiskies were often toxic in themselves, lager seemed like a great leap forward.

Lagering changed more than the beer. Mechanical refrigeration, which became available in the 1870s, made lager brewing possible year-round. The intense capital requirements of building and maintaining a large refrigeration plant drove many small brewers out of business and caused many more to consolidate into the several mega-brewing companies that dominate today. In their fight for outlets, these brewers bought up or otherwise controlled saloons that then had to serve only their beer. (These captive saloons are called "tied houses" and although they are outlawed in the United States, they are now the norm in the United Kingdom.)

The growth of huge breweries depended on equally large distribution systems. The railroads and motorized trucking enabled a brewer to sell beer far from its brewery. Advertising and promotion, funded by the savings involved in large-scale brewing, enabled the emerging national brands to compete with the locals. There was sporadic resistance, of course, sparked by nativist American resentment against the foreign lager and nostalgia for good, decent American Ale, but it was hopeless. By 1911, no less an authority than Mark Twain was using the word lager as a synonym for beer.

Competition between the giants came to mean price competition and promotion wars. By 1900, 86 percent of the beer produced in this country was in the light pilsner style, which was the cheapest to make and the most neutral tasting. The industry flowered, but the beer withered.

Its sorry history in America notwithstanding, there are many worthy lager styles: look for examples in the next chapter.

There are a few more defining provisions of the Federal Alcohol Administration Act. Here's one of my favorites.

No product containing less than one-half of one percent of alcohol by volume shall bear the class designations "beer," "lager beer," "lager," "ale," "porter," or "stout" or any other … designation commonly applied to malt beverages containing one-half of one percent or more of alcohol by volume.

Here's one that's violated as often as it's honored.

No product other than a malt beverage fermented at comparatively high temperature, possessing the characteristics generally attributed to "ale," "porter," or "stout" and produced without the use of coloring or flavoring materials (other than those recognized in standard brewing practices) shall bear any of these class designations.

In addition, geographic names are prohibited unless the beer comes from the place that's named on the label. Exceptions are made when the name has come to be generic (like India Pale Ale) or in two special cases. "Pilsen" and "Pilsner" can be used freely by American brewers if the beer conforms to that beer style, and "Bohemian" seems to have lost its status as an adjective of place. Subliminal advertising is also forbidden by the Federal Code: all those signs in the background at televised sporting events must therefore be something else.

Some Other Terms Frequently Bandied

ABV
The initials stand for Alcohol by Volume and are the standard measure of alcoholic strength on beer labels.

Bière de garde
This is beer that, contrary to the usual primacy of freshness, has been or should be aged before drinking, because it was made in win-

ter for summer consumption. This French term, the original property of the French and Belgians, is now used freely by writers to describe any beer that has the level of alcohol and intensity of flavor to improve with age.

Bottles

Most beer in colonial times was stored in barrels, and bottles remained a rarity until the 1870s, when Adolphus Busch started the large-scale distribution of bottled beer. His beer didn't spoil away from the coolness of the cellar, because of a combination of scrupulous cleanliness and pasteurization as part of his brewing technique.

The volume that made bottling feasible was made possible by a huge wave of immigration from beer-drinking countries and the marketing effort that Busch and other brewers put into courting the immigrants' business. At the same time, bottling for the home trade was a way to skirt local prohibition laws and anti-saloon sentiment. Bottled beer could be sold in the respectable atmosphere of drug and grocery stores. It could be transported home, even if home was in a "dry" jurisdiction.

Bottled beer was more than an evasionary convenience. Bottling accelerated brand identification and the entry of beer into retail outlets.

A bottle does two things for its beer. It keeps the beer in and it keeps light out. Light attacks beer and makes it stink. What happens is that light of a particular wavelength (below 550 nanometers if you must know) attacks the hops. When it does, it forms a chemical called mercaptan, which is the same stuff they put into natural gas to make it smell bad. Beer that's been light-struck is said to be "skunky." The skunks have decried the comparison.

Bottle-Conditioned Beer

See Cork-Finished Magnum

Cask-Conditioned Ale

This is unpasteurized beer that is carbonated in the individual cask or keg. It's usually dispensed by a hand pump without the pressure of CO_2 or nitrogen. Because cask-conditioned ale comes in contact with air once the keg is breached, the flavor changes from day to day. Cask Ale is sometimes referred to as "Real Ale" since the method is more traditional.

If you find yourself in love with cask ales, there are several cask-ale festivals in the US and UK.

Colors

As we've already seen, color is a pretty unreliable indicator of beer flavor. But there was a period of time, early in the craft-beer movement, when brewpubs in particular were just exploring the use of specialty malts and high hopping rates. These techniques gave the beer a color that was darker than the commercial lagers that everybody knew about, and a style with some extra caramel malt called Amber was created. There are a few "reds" out there too, and a couple of "browns." You can expect a red to be just a bit sweet and a brown to have toasty notes, but don't count on it.

Cork-Finished Magnum

Most breweries carbonate their beer by exposing it to compressed CO_2 as the beer is held in large, refrigerated stainless steel tanks. It's also possible to get the bubbles in there with the same technique used in Champagne. Each bottle gets a small dose of added sugar or malt syrup and perhaps a booster shot of yeast. The bottle is then closed, and the fermentation that takes place gives off CO_2, which is trapped in the bottle. The size most frequently chosen is the standard wine bottle (750ml), but occasionally these beers are bottled in Magnum (1.5L) or larger sizes.

These beers are often closed (finished) with a cork and wire closure like a Champagne bottle and the beer allowed to condition in the bottle. Unlike most other beers and Non-Vintage Champagne, cork-finished beers can improve with aging. Many beer lovers consider bottle-conditioned beers to be superior to draft versions of the same beer.

Double/Dubbel

This designation that appears on beer labels merely suggests that the beer in question is a higher-alcohol, thicker-bodied version of the style in question. So a Double Pale Ale should taste like a Pale Ale that's put on a few pounds.

If the word appears as an unmodified noun, it's probably referring to a particular style of beer. See Trappist in the next chapter.

Draft Beer

Once upon a time, all beer that wasn't homemade was draft beer: it was drawn from a keg and served within a few days of the keg's being broached. It had a short shelf life: beer that wasn't used up went sour. This beer had to be kept cool at all times. When we talk about draft beer today, the expression has two different senses, both derived from this earlier situation.

First, draft beer means "beer that is drawn from a keg." Its second meaning is "beer that's unpasteurized." The two meanings used to always coincide and today they don't. It's possible (and permitted under law) to put unpasteurized beer in a bottle and call it draft beer. It's just as possible for pasteurized beer to be put in a keg, drawn out and legally called draft beer.

In the 1950s, when most taverns still sold most of their beer on tap, there was a certain cachet to draft beer. Somehow it was closer to the source and more authentic. Pasteurization was tough on flavor, so draft certainly tasted better than the same brands served from bottles or cans.

Draft beer systems require a certain amount of skill to maintain, and by the 80s, with sales declining, fewer places were willing and able to maintain them properly. Draft beers from dirty lines were often the worst tasting alternative in a tavern, even if they were the cheapest. All the full-flavored imports came in bottles, and consumers had become used to the pasteurized version of American product sold in grocery stores.

But draft beer has one powerful advantage that couldn't be denied for long: packaging costs are low, so draft beer is very cheap to buy and very profitable to serve. Draft had to come back and it did. The new brewpubs could hardly afford the expense of bottling, and imported beers started showing up in kegs. Some of the kegs were even unpasteurized. Increased competition set the mega-breweries to training their customers in the use of draft equipment. All of a sudden, bars are advertising the number of taps they have.

In 1950, 28 percent of the beer sold in America was draft beer. By 1991, that figure had slipped to 11 percent. Since almost all draft beer is sold in taverns, this number is in part a reflection of the decline of taverns as social and business institutions. In the United Kingdom, by contrast, 71 percent of beer is served on draft.

Export

The roots of this beer label word lie in the actual export of German or English beers, the exported versions being assumed to be higher in quality and fuller in alcohol. Today, the word is merely a stylistic device, like Napoleon on a Cognac label.

Green Beer

This is beer that's fresh from the fermenter, unaged, unlagered and generally uninterfered with. It has a way to go before it becomes drinkable beer; a week to two if it's an ale, several weeks more than that if it's a lager. If, on any particular ethnic holiday, someone offers you a green beer, you should ask her if she means beer that fits this description. If she says yes, Dr. Manners suggests that you reply that you really prefer properly matured beer but thanks so much for the offer. If on the other hand, gentle reader, she is offering you beer that, in defiance of Nature and Nature's laws, has been chemically dyed to look green, then you must put down your glass, put on your Viking helmet and proceed to loot, pillage and burn. Tipping is not required.

Growler

A growler is a jug, often with an attached lid, that is used as a take-out container in jurisdictions where such things are legal. Before the widespread use of bottles and cans, a growler was the only way to consume beer at home. Some saloons had separate and discreet entrances for ladies who wished to take home a growler.

Hoppy

A word used to describe beers whose dominant flavors are derived from hops, either in the form of bitter tastes or herbal, spicy or flowery aromas. American beer these days is sporting a lot of hop aromas that resemble citrus fruits, especially grapefruit.

Mead

Unless you went to a college that made you read *Beowulf* or Njal's saga, there's really no reason you should have heard about mead. Mead is an alcoholic drink made from a fermented solution of honey and water.

In most parts of the world, grapes or grain were much cheaper sources of fermentable sugar. Honey was more likely to be reserved for cooking or licking off eager fingers. In the few places where there was no barley to be malted and fermented into beer, or grape juice to ferment itself into wine, you could still make a drink from honey. You could think of mead as a honey wine, although it's closer in strength and spirit to beer.

Honey was expensive because the honey gatherer had to endure the stings of angry wild bees to collect it. Even when bees were domesticated, a hive had to be burned (and all the bees killed) to gather honey. In a world with a shortage of sweeteners and an abundance of fermentable material, mead making was not a very worthwhile project.

Of course, on the fringes of the civilized world where climate was too harsh for grapes or barley, mead was prized indeed. In pre-Norman Wales it was valued at two to four times the price of ale. It was the Vikings and Britons who made and enjoyed mead. The drink remained popular in Britain until the time of Henry VIII.

Mead is associated then with some of history's least couth bad boys. But that alone isn't reason enough to make it. A better reason is that honey is available all year-round and is an extremely versatile way of producing your first homebrew. You can, through a combination of fruits and spices, make a drink that's exactly to your taste and is distinctively your own. Unlike beer making proper, lengthy boiling is not required

Mead making is also very reliable. You can join the movement toward high-touch, homemade products and have a great chance of success. Your homemade bread may feel like a doorstop and canning your own anything may look too much like botulism, but your mead is almost certain to be delicious. Every mead I've tasted was at its best when served around 50°F.

Malty

Of course, every good beer is made from malted barley, so what do we mean when we use the word as an adjective to describe the taste of a particular beer? We're saying that the beer in question has a predominance of cereal flavors. Usually these also translate into a thickness in the mouth and suggestions of sweetness.

Mock Premium

Mock premium beer is a cheap product that's been repackaged to look expensive with no substantive additions to the actual beer.

Mock premium had a brief period of growth, but sales in America have stopped growing. Even the expanding population isn't helping. The only categories of real beer that are increasing their sales each year are imports and craft-brewed beers. Naturally enough, the largest brewers are jealously eyeing that sales growth and hoping to get in on the action, or at least forestall desertions from their product line. In order to cash in, they have created beer containers with the graphic feel of beer-with-flavor. Mock premium brands look like imports or American microbrews. German names help sell beer; Irish names are even better.

I take this development as a very encouraging sign. First it shows that the giants are acknowledging the impact of good beer in the market place. It also shows that they are able to pay careful attention to the exterior attributes of the craft beers and produce visually plausible entries into the category.

There's just one thing left to do. They have to improve the beer itself. (Right now, the mock premiums are only just distinguishable from their regular offerings.) We know they can do it; there are some very good brewers out there. Some of them are, no doubt, as good as the marketers who thought up the names.

Nitrogen
Nitrogen doesn't dissolve in beer as readily as CO_2 does. When it's used to pressurize and transport beer, a small amount dissolves under pressure in the beer. When the beer is dispensed, the bubbles rush out of solution as soon as they form. Because they come out of solution so quickly, they are smaller than CO_2 bubbles. These smaller bubbles give a thicker, more creamy consistency to the beer. Some beers, notably Guinness Extra Stout, use nitrogen as an important part of their presentation.

Non-alcoholic (NA)
NA beers are something of an oxymoron. Even government reg-

ulations allow that for something to be called beer it must contain at least 0.5 percent alcohol. Products that can be sold as no- or low-alcohol beers can be produced in four ways.

1. You can make up a traditional beer wort with malt sugars and hops and then not ferment it (or ferment it very slightly). Since you're stuck with all or almost all the sugar you start out with, the approach yields two types of beer. You can either make a very sweet drink that's analogous to soda pop, or one that is only slightly sweet with just enough hops to balance the malt.

2. You can make a regular beer, distill out the alcohol, add back the flavors that are lost up the still pipe, and recarbonate.

3. You can make a regular beer and then remove the alcohol through an osmotic membrane. This process is akin to dialysis and the beer produced this way is said to go well with steak and kidney pie.

4. You can prepare a regular beer and ferment it out with a mutant yeast that doesn't produce any alcohol.

At this writing, no one has figured out how to restore balance to a beer without alcohol. There are no traditional beer styles without alcohol and worse yet, all the NA beers end up being compared to real beer.

Today's non-alcoholic beers are alternatives for beer drinkers when alcohol is an inconvenient or inappropriate drink. They also appeal to people who, for one reason or another, never drink real beer, but would like to be reminded of the taste of beer or enjoy the sociability of beer-drinking environments. NA beers are the distant cousins of the "near beers" that were produced during prohibition. Of near beer it was said that whoever named them was a very poor judge of distance. The situation has improved slightly.

Non-alcoholic beers account for just over 1 percent of beer sales in the US and about 5 percent in Europe.

Off-Dry

This term is borrowed from wine-speak where it means that a wine is just barely detectably sweet. In beer land, the sense is a little bit different. It suggests that in the balance between malty-sweet and hoppy-bitter flavor, the sweet ones are allowed to play a more prominent role, and the sensation of the beer is more centered on its malt than its hops.

Pint

You probably won't be surprised to learn that a pint is a measure containing sixteen fluid ounces in the US and twenty fluid ounces in the UK. What you may not know is that our English cousins consider their pint to be the right and proper measure for beer. If the beer is good, as theirs often is, they may have a point. They are so certain of this that they use "a pint" as a synonym for beer consumed in a tavern.

Plimsoll Line

This is the facetious English name for the line etched on a beer glass to mark a full measure. The reference is to the series of lines seen on the side of cargo ships that indicate maximum loading levels.

Pony

A small glass or a small portion of beer, somewhere between three and seven ounces. By extension, a very small keg that a private host might buy for a party.

Rauchbier

Malt used to be toasted over open fires and the smoke from the fire necessarily flavored the malt, which added a smoky flavor to the beer. Development of more efficient ovens and rotary roasters helped malt give up smoking, but a few rauchbiers (*rauch* is the German word for smoke) still recollect the original wood fire. Rauchbier can be either ale or lager. The trick in brewing them is to keep the smoky flavors in check and to balance them with some other characteristic. The brewers of Bamberg, Germany, do the most with the style but the production is small.

- Sly Fox Rauchbier solves the problem of balance with a round, fruity taste. Only at the finish does the smoke come to dominate the flavor.
- Baron Rauchbier from Seattle goes light on the smoke and achieves its balance with a pleasant meaty flavor. Perfect for those moments when you feel like drinking a sausage.
- Triumph Rauchweizen puts up spicy aromas and malty banana flavors against a small dose of smoke.

Roasted

What a strange word to use to describe something as obviously wet and unroastable as beer. The word is, nonetheless, unavoidable and accurate. Careful attention to the taste of beer will force you to notice tastes that remind you of toasted bread and roasted grain. The source of these flavors is the roasting of the malted grain. The chemistry behind this flavor is the same thing that's responsible for the color and flavor of bread crust, chocolate and coffee. It's a series of events called the Maillard Reactions (one of which is the candy maker's friend: caramelization).

It all begins when a sugar molecule reacts with the nitrogen part of an amino acid. The two form an unstable alliance that falls apart, leaving a lot of intensely flavorful compounds and a brown color in its wake. These reactions happen mostly at high temperatures—well above the boiling point of water—but well within the range of the malt-roasting oven.

Saccharomyces

The word means sugar mushrooms and it is the scientific name of the yeast that does the work of fermentation.

Sake

Sake (often mispronounced as sa-kee, rather than sa-keh) is properly a beer because it is made by fermenting sugar derived from grain. The Japanese method for converting rice starch into sugar uses enzymes from a mold that grows on the rice and would, if left alone, convert the starch to sugar for its own use. Yeast is introduced at the same time that the conversion to sugar is happening and both processes go on simultaneously. Sake once dominated the Japanese market so thoroughly that the word is a synonym for alcoholic beverage. Sake is almost always over 12 percent alcohol and is used like a wine.

Sedimented

A very few beers are handled like champagne. After fermentation, they are bottled with a small dose of fresh sugar and yeast and allowed to ferment a second time in the bottle. The second fermentation carbonates the beer and leaves a sediment of yeast behind in the bottle. A few devotees shake their beer to make sure they get all of the yeast and all of its Vitamin B.

To pour a sedimented beer without getting yeast in your glass, let the bottle stand upright for a few hours until the yeast settles to the bottom and the beer looks clear. Pour the beer in one continuous pour: if the bottle is oversized, you may want to pour into a pitcher and then into several glasses. If you get some yeast in one of the glasses, drink it anyway. Tell your drinking companions that you think clarity is highly overrated as a quality in beer and you, for one, prefer the subtle, "bake-shop" note that yeast adds to the bouquet. The best way to keep a straight face in the midst of these declarations is to have another sip.

Sessions Beer

Beer that's low in alcohol and suitable for a long session of drinking. The expression is British, but the custom is widespread.

Six-Pack

In adolescent folklore at least, the "six" is the standard unit of beer consumption. There are just over fifty-five six-packs in a barrel. The six-pack was developed by the soft drink industry during Prohibition. It represented a balance between the soft drink manufacturers' desire to sell the maximum number of bottles at one time and the weight that most women shoppers were comfortable carrying.

After Prohibition, these same brewers were back in the beer business and anxious to cultivate the home market. They had the same considerations of scale and weight. They were also able to take advantage of a buying habit that the soft drink bottlers had cultivated. The first six-packs appeared in 1933. They were impenetrable fortresses; sealed boxes that protected and insulated the bottles inside.

Curiously, in the early years of the twenty-first century, "six-pack" has been a descriptor of a tightly muscled abdomen; exactly the sort of anatomical structure unlikely to be found on people consuming lots of six-packs.

Summer Beers

It was the kind of heat wave that killed the dinosaurs. It was heat that dragged the wetness down your throat and into your lungs and threatened to drown you. More bad news; nothing helped. Sweating didn't make you cool, it just made you sweaty.

A cold glass of water just made you feel bloated and sinking into the heat. A cool piece of fruit reminded you of an apple stuck in a roast pig's mouth. Your earth-conscious fan only blew nauseous waves of heat at you more efficiently. Your tiny air-conditioner seemed to be suffering as much as you were, and the stale stink of the unmoving air outdoors got worse by the minute as more small creatures were killed by and then braised in the sulfurous heat and trapped machine fumes.

And then finally you reach for television's solution to parched person. You go for a cold one. Gimme a frosty. It's a brewski for youski, Bubba. Out of the warm and into the cold, clean taste of—a sick watery sourness that left a bad taste in your mouth that you somehow never noticed before. In fact you maybe never even have noticed how beer tasted before. Nothing like global warming cooking up the heat wave of the century to make a beer maven out of you, eh?

So the really bad news is that the TV commercials lied to you. The pissy bitterness of your usual beer was somehow unsatisfying. It was still less filling, but it certainly didn't taste great. In fact, you were shocked that you noticed the taste at all. What is this stuff anyway, and why are you drinking it? Why are those people over there drinking beer and smacking their lips? Smacking of lips is rude. Reminding you that you're habituated to drinking something that's either bad-tasting or non-tasting is even ruder. Rudest of all is not offering you one of whatever they're having.

What they're having might be something that has a medium amount of flavor in a beer without a lot of malty heaviness. It may also be a beer that has a hint of sourness in its finish rather than the usual sweet overtones. Acidy tastes are tried and true thirst quenchers; otherwise, why would we bother with the paradox of lemon juice and sugar to make lemonade?

Chances are good that their delicious summer beer is a beer that's low in alcohol too. Alcohol steals water from your cells, and the object of this game is to put water back in you. Beers made with a portion of wheat usually have both these qualities, as the number of wheat (weisse/white) beers named below indicates.

Here are a few beers worth trying in hot weather:

• Saison Dupont, Belgian farmhouse ale, spicy and fruity with a long, dry finish: it reminds a bit of Champagne and appears on a lot of Ten Best Lists

  • Schneider Aventinus: rich and light

  • Hoegaarden, the wonderful wheaty Ho, of course

  • Allagash White, slightly eccentric flavors that ends with a beautiful citrusy finish

- St. Bernardus Blanche, bottle-conditioned, creamy, spicy with a huge head that seems to blow citrus aromas in your face

Wassail

The wassail bowl is an English holiday tradition involving mixing (unhopped) ale with fruits, spices and toast in a large bowl and passing the bowl around the company. Before you reject the idea of spicing your beer, remember that the ale in question was unhopped and probably gained a lot by being spiced. Here, excerpted from John Bickerdyke, is a recipe from Oxford University, where apparently they know best about such things.

> Into a bowl, place half a pound of Lisbon sugar, on which is poured one pint of warm beer. Some nutmeg and ginger are then grated over the mixture, and four glasses of sherry (?) and five pints of beer are added to it. It is then stirred, sweetened to taste and allowed to stand covered up for two or three hours. Three or four slices of thin toast are then floated on the creaming mixture and the wassail bowl is ready. Sometimes a couple or three slices of lemon and a few lumps of sugar rubbed on the peeling of a lemon are introduced.

The slang term for this beverage at Oxford was "Swig." Do you think that they put enough sugar in it? A variation called for the hot mixture to be poured over roasted apples.

Wassail was one example of a larger tradition called "ale cups." There were scores of local recipes and holiday variations. They were usually made in generous quantity and so invited a large company to drink them. More than anything else, hops in beer killed them off. If there are any prospects for the return of ale cups in general and wassail in particular, they lie with lightly hopped wheat beers as bases.

Winter Beers

Here's an example of a category of beer that is a long way from representing a style or a group of recipes. These are beers that rise to a particular climatic occasion. In the days before refrigeration, the cooler months were the best time to brew beer. The tradition of brewing a special beer to mark the winter solstice gradually grew into a tradition of making thicker, sweeter, maltier beers. These brews supplied the extra calories that are required to keep up one's body heat and a bit of extra alcohol to keep up one's mood.

There are enough beers brewed today to keep the cold at bay that Winter Beer Festivals are springing up. Here are a few beers to look for.

- Hoppy the Woodsman is one of the few winter beers that leads with its hops aroma. It is remarkably smooth with a Bourbon nose.
- Anchor Christmas Ale is available from November to January. Each year's batch is differently spiced, but they always have medium alcohol—around 5.5%—and a charming maltiness.
- Mackeson XXX Stout is a low-alcohol, high-flavor black beer with aromas of caramel, coffee and chocolate. It finishes slightly sweet with a hint of licorice.
- Gouden Carolus Noel ("Golden Charlie") sports an intoxicatingly balanced mix of spices, nutmeg and clove that weaves its way through a palate of figs and plums. Cocoa in the finish. Both rich and light at the same time, it comes in a Magnum, cork-finished bottle.

X

X shows up on a lot of beer labels, sometimes in the company of one or two other Xs. This has nothing to do with X-rated movies or with X marking the spot. The practice may have originated with a British law of 1531 that required barrels of legal capacity to be marked with the "sign and token of St. Anthony's cross." St.

A selection of Trappist and Abbey ales.

Anthony's cross looks like an X laid on its side. A better story has it that the Xs enabled illiterate brewery workers to distinguish grades of ale; Simplex (single X) Duplex (XX) and Triplex (XXX). The Xs don't signify multipliers. XX is not twice as strong as X, it's merely the next grade up. Double (dubble) and Triple (tripple) survive as informal names for the strongest Belgian Trappist ales (both of which constitute a family of beers if not a style) and XX (Dos Equis) is a very successful Mexican dark lager.

Yard of Ale

This trumpet-shaped glass has a narrow end formed into a ball. The "yard" usually stands in its own supporting rack. Older sources give its capacity as just over a pint, but modern versions are in the forty- to fifty-ounce range. The glass's reason for being lies in the rounded bottom. Impossible to set down, it must be drained in one long pull. Aside from the amount of beer involved, the sudden surge of liquid when the drinker reaches the beer in the bottom makes the feat difficult.

The ale yard served as an initiation rite at English public schools, which may give you an idea of the spirit of the thing. Expressions like "sado-masochistic" and "trial-by-gullet" come to mind. Standing behind a bar, watching a soon-to-be bridegroom throw down an evening's worth of beer in a single pull as all his friends cheer him on is enough to put you off drinking for a week.

Discussion Questions
1. Do any of these terms help you get a handle on some experience you've already had with beer?
2. Can you construct a plausible observation about beer, using any three of the terms listed above, in the same sentence? Can you do it with a straight face?

Chapter 7

A Dictionary of Beer Styles

After reading this chapter, you will be able to
- navigate your way through many of the confusing terms on modern beer labels
- look at a twenty-page beer list and smile
- discourse knowledgeably, when knowledgeable discourse is appropriate
- have a few beers to look forward to

Identity Standards

The Federal Alcohol Administration Act of 1935 gives the Bureau of Alcohol, Tobacco, Firearms (BATF) the authority to "regulate the labeling and advertising of ... malt beverages." The law allows the Bureau to issue regulations to "prohibit deception of the customer with respect to the product and which will provide the customer with adequate information as to the identity and quality of the product."

The closest the Act comes to defining anything is this:

> Malt beverage: a beverage made by the alcoholic fermentation of an infusion or decoction, or combination of both (see mashing) in potable brewing water, of malted barley with hops, or their parts, or their products, and with or without other malted cereals, other carbohydrates or products prepared therefrom, and with or without the addition of carbon dioxide, and with or without other wholesome products suitable for human food consumption.

Beer Styles

There are about eight thousand breweries in the world, maybe five or six different beers brewed in each one. That's forty-eight thousand different labels. How does a novice beer enthusiast make sense of it all? The recipe, that's how. Wine is pretty easy to understand. European wines are named for the place where the grapes are grown: Bordeaux, Barolo; American wines for the grape they come from: Chardonnay, Zinfandel. The names smell of geography, botany and romance. They tell you what to expect.

Beer is different. Beer is usually named for the brewer or his town or his hero. Adolf Coors, Peter Ballantine, Budweis, Bohemia, St. Sixtus. Brand names trying to make their way in the world, they are commercial fermentations competing for your attention. Brand names are supposed to excite the consumer, not inform the connoisseur. If you want to find out what a beer is all about, one way is to taste it and understand the brewer's recipe. Similar beers with similar recipes are grouped together and spoken of as a "style." How many styles are there? The American Homebrewers' Association lists 140 different styles in their current guide, but even that number doesn't express the diversity of tastes in the world of beer.

We can make it a bit easier if we remember that there are two broad categories of beer styles: the first and oldest are ales, the newfangled ones are the lagers.

Individual styles (and sometimes groups of styles) have their own entries in this book. Just keep in mind that most descriptions of beer are references to style and that styles are nothing more than recipes. Recipes spell out which malts, hops, water and yeast are used. They also specify how much alcohol and unfermented sugar will be in the final beer. Many people feel that the individual strain of yeast used in fermentation is the most important factor in determining the flavor of a style.

Some lager styles are: Bock, Munich, Pils, Dortmunder, High-gravity Lagers, American Pilsner, Malt Liquor.

Some ale styles are: Wheat beer, Lambics, Stout, Porter, Fruit Beers, Mead and Honey Beer, Kölsch, Strong Ales, English Ale,

Brown Ale, Trappist.

Like any set of categories outside pure mathematics, the divisions are imprecise and overlapping. They are also not the only possible categories for the world of beer. We could just as easily categorize beers by geography or alcohol or residual sweetness. No matter: the purpose of a good categorization is not simply to divide up the world of beer, but to say something useful. In this case, we make categories to give the enthusiast some idea of what is in store. Remember too that styles are only generalizations about recipes. It's possible to create a beer recipe that doesn't fit precisely into the definition of any particular style.

Beer styles as proclaimed on beer labels are not always reliable indicators of what's in the bottle. There are no national standards of identity for beer in this country. Local standards are a hodgepodge. I have adopted the practice of taking each label at its face value and including in the critical comments on a style, any beers that proclaim themselves in that style.

Ales

Abbey beer isn't made in a monastery, but it tastes a lot like beers that are. Whether they're made in Belgium or not, abbey beers have names that pay homage to or make gentle fun of the Trappist beers. Some abbey beers are contract-brewed for monastic establishments that don't brew but would support themselves in the beer trade. Abbey isn't strictly a style, as recipes vary, but they tend to imitate the Trappist practice of having a dark and richly flavored dubbel and a spicy and intense tripel, both of which are bottle-conditioned. They are intended to be served at cellar temperature. If you live in an apartment, let me remind you that cellars run about 60°F/16C.

• Allagash Brewery in Portland, Maine, makes a splendid tripel with honey and banana on the palate and a fruit and herb nose: extremely versatile with food. Look for it in a cork-finished 750ml bottle. They also have a perfectly made dubbel.

• La Rulles from Belgium is a tripel with a subtly layered set of malty flavors interwoven with a light bitterness. Superb.

Altbier is a traditional German style of ale that predates the rise of lagering. The German word *alt* means old, and these beers use the older, top-fermenting, ale yeasts. The flavor is ale-like too; they have a copper color, a lot of hops and a bittersweet caramel and citrus flavor.

It used to be hard to find bottled examples, so you were most likely to run into this delightful beer at a brewpub or from a home-brewer. A related, lighter style is Kölsch. Serve Altbier around 50°F/14C.

• Schlussel Alt is 5% alcohol and the bottled version is available. It is the epitome of perfect balance in a beer. You should try it next to one of the 5% lagers that are popular in the US.

• McNeills Alle Tage Altbier from Vermont shows up in a 22 oz (660ml) bottle which seems like the right portion. This hazy amber beer has a toffee and caramel taste with a floral hops, a flavor that's underplayed and balanced.

Barley wine is not a contradiction in terms. It's more like a play on words. Barley wines are beers that are made to the same alcohol level as wines and are usually aged for a few months. There are even barley wines that are dated when they're brewed then "put down" to age in bottles for years, and are said to improve in the process.

Some very few have an actual wine-like taste; most have a spicy and very dense-tasting maltiness with a long finish. Alcohol levels aside, a small glass of intensely flavored barley wine goes a long way. Brewpubs that serve it usually keep a special smaller glass for the purpose and some brewers bottle it in smaller-than-usual bottles. In the US, the authorities are afraid you may confuse Old Foghorn with Vieux Telegraphe, and so the term "barley wine" is forbidden and the more euphonious "barley wine–style ale" substituted.

Some authorities suggest serving barley wine at room temperature. I haven't met one yet that couldn't be improved by a slight chill down to about 60°F/16C.

- Thomas Hardy's Ale reviewed below
- Old Nick from Young's follows the American standard and describes itself as a barley wine–style ale. It's reddish in color, pleasantly bitter with a long caramel finish. Lighter and less alcoholic than real barley wines, it still gives a good impression of the style.
- Old Foghorn is probably America's best barley wine. It has a deep, scrumptious malty complexity, leavened by an exuberant hoppy nose. My most recent tastings had a distinct black pepper and alcohol aroma that seemed best in a snifter. 8.8%
- Old Horizontal is one of the most beautiful dark beers: a deep dark red that puts you in mind of a gem stone. Malt, fruit, and rum, well-balanced hoppiness and a surprisingly dry and smooth finish. There's a bit of booziness at 10% ABV.

Bitter brings to mind the transparently wonderful story of Dunkirk: a fleet of small boats manned by English civilians crosses the choppy waters of the English Channel to rescue soldiers stranded and pressed by German fire on the beaches of Dunkirk on the coast of France. It's worth a book, it's worth a movie, it's even worth an opera.

The only time since Dunkirk that the British public has been roused to a similar generous, public-spirited action is in defense of their fruity and hoppy ales, which are known colloquially as bitter. The name is apt; these are beers that emphasize the bitter characteristic of the hops and downplay or ignore the aromatic side.

CAMRA (The Campaign for Real Ale) is a British consumer movement that started in 1971 in response to the dwindling availability of cask-conditioned bitter. They sponsor the Great British Beer Festival and publish a newsletter called *What's Brewing* and a serious pub tour guide called the *Good Beer Guide*.

Real bitter is primarily a draft product for service in pubs. Properly, bitter is served from a wooden cask, in which it develops and from which it is drawn by a pump. Less than ideal, but still lovable, is bitter served from kegs. Kegged English beer is available but still scarce in this country. Fortunately, there are some bottled examples that can give us a sense of the real thing.

- Fuller's ESB (Extra Special Bitter) has a complex, sour malty nose, a load of hops and a finish with a surprising and delightful sweetness. A Grand Canyon of a beer, with a place on my personal Ten Best List. ESB has come to stand for any English brewery's richest offering.
- Yard's ESA (Extra Special Ale) is a balanced tribute to the British style that was originally brewed and is still sometimes available as a cask-conditioned ale. The ESA in the name is both a tribute to and a pun on ESB.

> The Anglo-Saxons consumed beer on an oceanic scale.
> H.P.R. Finberg

Burton ale is a pale bitter made in the town of Burton-on-Trent, England. The beer is made from water that is very high in minerals. The mineralization of the water is noticeable in the ale. Some people claim that a glass of Burton leaves a ring around your mouth. Some of its devotees refer to it, with no apparent rancor, as Old Kidney Stone. Burton salts are available to the homebrewer who wants to experiment with the style.

Burton-on-Trent is also the home of the first India Pale Ales or IPA.

- Double Diamond Burton Ale has a hard edge in the mouth that makes the mineral analysis believable. The edge is in balance with an aromatic, late afternoon charm. The draft versions were

far superior to the bottled and worth looking for.
- Galbraith Old Burton Pale Ale from New Zealand. This 6.6% alcohol ale is worth seeking out. The floral hoppiness creates a perfect balance with the tangy minerality.

Cream ale is a light-bodied, sweet style of ale, enjoyed for its thirst-quenching properties. Most recipes for cream ale call for the addition of corn sugar to the wort. The sugar lightens the body and reduces the flavor (and cost) while keeping the alcohol content in the usual range of beer. If you extend this thinking much further, the sugary tail starts to wag the malty dog and you end up with malt liquor. Some of the cream ales I've tasted have been refreshing, some have been cloying and childish: none was particularly worth mentioning. Serve below 50°F.

Duvel—I'm not sure that I ought to tell you about Duvel. After all, we've scarcely met, and this beer is hard enough to find as it is. On the other hand, if there's a run on Duvel, maybe the other brewers will notice and try to do better.

Duvel is a brand, a yeasty and full-bodied Belgian beer with a honey-like color and plummy bouquet. It is luscious and refreshing and deceptively high in alcohol. The style could be called Belgian Strong Ale, but Duvel has almost become a style of its own. Unfortunately, variability from bottle to bottle is high, at least in this country. Occasionally on tap, the best Duvel seems to come in cork-finished 750ml bottles. Serve between 45° and 50°F.

The brewers of Duvel are now brewing at the Ommegang Brewery in Cooperstown, New York.

Farmhouse (Saison) is usually described with the words spice, grass and barnyard, an earthy, elegant beer derived from a Belgian style that was brewed in the winter to be enjoyed in the summer.
- The dean of farmhouse ales—in fact the very definition—is

Saison Dupont (Vielle Provision). It has all the characteristics of the style plus a bit of new-mown hay. It has a spectacularly long and lovely finish.

- Lost Abbey Brouwers Imagination Series Saison is a stronger version of the style with a hint of sweetness, a suggestion of honey and a fair amount of yeast and grassiness. (Note the word "brouwers." It's the Flemish word for brewer and part of the tribute that American craft brewing is paying to its Belgian roots.)
- Fantôme Saison is a high ABV (8%) farmhouse, fruity and acidic with a Riesling-like finish: hard to find and definitely worth the hunt.
- Smuttynose Farmhouse from Hampton, New Hampshire, is the best American example: earthy and peppery with a hint of sweetness. A work of genius that's only available seasonally.

Faro is a traditional Belgian style, low in alcohol and brewed for springtime drinking. Usually two beers were blended, a low gravity and a medium gravity. The blend was sweetened, which made it re-ferment and sparkle, watered and served as a quencher. Today a Faro is likely to be pasteurized, spiced and bottled. This degree of freedom makes for some adventurous tastes and beers that are easy to love.

- Boon Faro is a blend of aged gueuze and witbier. Fruity, rich and elegant, it's a beer to seek out, especially in warmer weather. From the pioneering Frank Boon in Lembeek, Belgium.
- 3 Fonteinen Faro is a complex, sweet-and-sour concoction with a musty base. Much more appetizing than it sounds.

Festbiers are traditional beers, usually high in alcohol, body and sweetness, that are brewed once a year to be drunk on a particular holiday or beer festival.

- The Bavarian Oktoberfest and its beers is probably the best known secular beer festival. It is celebrated (or used as a pro-motional device) all over the beer-drinking world.

Some religious holidays have their own beers

- Nochebuena is a malty Mexican Christmas beer. Mexico also brews Navidad and Commemorativa for the holiday.
- And then of course, there are Purim beers which are noted for their esters.

> 'Twas Christmas broached the mightiest ale;
> 'Twas Christmas told the merriest tale.
> —Sir Walter Scott

Framboise or Frambozen beers are made with the addition of raspberries. The base beer may be a lambic, a brown ale or a simple wheat beer. These are mostly Belgian and mostly wonderful. These are beers that are often proffered to folks who claim that they don't like beer. These people should be aware of the relatively high alcohols.

- Lindeman's Framboise is great and widely available. The taste is all raspberry with a slightly sour finish. The very low 2.5% alcohol makes it perfect with a salad at lunch.

Fruit beers—Why not? A beer made from a light malt, or one with a portion of wheat as an adjunct, can be a wonderful background for fruit flavor. Another possible base is a simple brown ale. Fruit can be added to the fermenting wort or pasteurized fruit syrup can be added to finished beer. Fruit beers are often a happy surprise to the "I don't like beer" crowd. I imagine that a fruit lager would be possible: there are lager-like beers spiked with citrus flavor. At the moment, most of the fruit beers are ales.

Grand Cru hasn't escaped from a wine book and fought its way over to this one. The word *cru* means harvest in French, but it has the additional meaning of a grade or classification. Grand Cru wines are ones made from grapes grown in vineyards that have been classified grand. In French wines, at least, the term can't be tossed around casually. Both law and public knowledge restrict its use. Outside of France and in the land of beer, things are quite different.

Several breweries now use the name Grand Cru, but the usages don't constitute a beer style. As it happens, a few of these beers are wonderful enough to call themselves grand.

- Rodenbach Grand Cru: did someone say Burgundy? This garnet-colored beer has an actual fruity complexity that rivals champagne.
- Allagash Grand Cru is a winter seasonal. Almost orange, the warmth of the color is echoed in the sherbety flavor.

Gueuze (GU zuh) is a toned-down, more accessible version of the lambic beer style. It's made by blending an older, sour lambic with some young stuff. The result is off-dry but loaded with fruit and very sophisticated. By all means, try any gueuze that you get your hands on, but look especially for one from Frank Boon.

India Pale Ale or **IPA** was originally brewed for British troops stationed in India in the eighteenth century. It was brewed very strong and heavily hopped to survive a boat ride that could last six months, and subsequent storage in a tropical climate. IPA is best bottled and with its wonderful excess of character has made a lot of converts from the ranks of American Pilsner drinkers.

India Pale Ale is an idea. The expression of the idea in England takes place in the context of English hop varieties and a tax system that penalizes, or at least charges for, more malt and more alcohol. There are compromises that result and the style is a reflection of them. In America, we have our own hop varieties, and while more malt costs more, there's no tax penalty. So being less constrained, we are more expansive. Cascades hops adds a fruity, grand-citrus aroma. Big malt and alcohol makes for a rich body and mouth feel. The best American IPAs are opulent and seductive. The best British IPAs are, in comparison, small, intricate and interesting.

- Ballantine India Pale Ale is a sentimental favorite. In the Brooklyn taprooms of my youth, most of the beer tasted like plastic tubing. Ballantine IPA was one of the few beers with flavor. We called it the Green Death. At that time, it was probably the bitterest commercial beer made in America. The most recent version was made by Falstaff Brewing Co. It had a warm, golden color that could pass, in the right light, for a sparkling blush Zinfandel.
- Dogfish Head 90 minute IPA: the forward impression is grapefruit and grass in the nose. If the beer is at the right serving temperature, you're hit with an almost unbelievable richness. Certainly one of the ten most delicious beers made in the United States.
- Flying Dog Snake Dog IPA: Here's an expression of hops as a citrus fruit: grapefruity, lemony and lots of fun.

Kölsch is the beer style native to Cologne, Germany. It is an ale, light in color and sometimes showing an acidic character. Some people, especially those raised on English and Belgian beer, consider this the most delightful German beer.

Kriekenbeer is a kind of fruit beer made from cherries and brown ale. Kriekenbier is much simpler in flavor than kriek lambic, and an easier taste to acquire.

- Verhaeghe Echte Kriek pours red with a pink head. Looking at it is almost as much fun as drinking it, but don't just stare: there's a lovely vanilla note hidden in the huge cherry-orchard aroma and a great balance between sweet and sour flavors on the palate. At almost 7% alcohol, it's almost too tasty.

Lambic is to beer what single malt Scotch is to whisky. It is a style that is exotically produced, expensive, sometimes difficult to like. It's made by small artisanal outfits in hard-to-find European country barns. It's difficult to find and worthy of endless conversations.

Lambic is a style of beer native to Belgium that depends on wild yeasts. Most brewers are very careful to introduce their own specially selected yeast to the sugary wort. When fermentation begins in their brewhouses, they know what flavor will result, in part because they know what yeast is in charge. These brewers run very efficient gardens where all the plants except the one they favor are weeded out.

Lambic brewers let nature take its course. They make their wort and leave the fermenter open for a micro-organismic free-for-all. Yeasts and bacteria are all encouraged to join in and contribute their flavor as they live on the sugar. Fermentation occurs in stages. First bacteria, then yeast, more yeasts and bacteria again take over. The entire first fermentation can take a year. Since each brewhouse collects its own unique collection of airborne flora, each lambic is different.

Some lambics have fruit added, others stand on the wild yeast flavor alone. The fruited beers are easy to like. The unfruited ones, with their sour, lactic acid flavor, are definitely an acquired taste.

The beers that are made this way may be aged, blended or dosed with fruit. They are almost always bottle-conditioned and closed with a cork and wire basket.

- A wonderful palate cleanser and champagne stand-in is the Belgian Framboise Lambic from Lindemann's ($7). It tastes exactly like a perfectly dry and very fresh carbonated raspberry.
- I have to pass on Kriek Lambic, which is another fruit beer based on cherries. It bears an uncanny resemblance to the flavor used to mask the cough medicines of my youth. While not

exactly unpleasant, it is distracting. Whenever I taste one, I find myself looking for someone to hand me a hot water bottle or try to take my temperature.

Mild is an English style; lighter, sweeter and less alcoholic than bitter. Mild is intended to be served on draft. In America, "mild" is not a good word with which to sell beer, so examples of the style often have hyper-macho names. One of my favorite homebrew versions was called Knuckle Buster. This is a style much beloved of brewpubs who appreciate the fact that it's less expensive to make and that they don't have to store it for long before service. You'll find a lot of milds on tap and only a few in bottles.
- Brawler, a lightly carameled and thirst-quenching beer just under 5% ABV whose advertising copy claims that it's a "malt-forward, ruby colored ale … great for when you want to go a few rounds."

Nut brown ale is the color of the skin on a filbert, a rich mahogany. Flavors are gently understated, and this beer is often mentioned as a suitable introduction to beer for people who don't know how much they like it.
- Samuel Smith's Nut Brown Ale: slightly spicy, light-bodied with a substantial bitterness. In draft beer form, it seems maltier and barely carbonated
- Newcastle: light-bodied, pleasantly malty with a barely bitter finish, this is a pleasant beer that would be a lot more enjoyable if it were sold at about two-thirds its current price.

Pale ale is by modern standards not particularly pale. The paleness was noted in contrast to the darker, cloudy styles that preceded it. Pale ales were among the first to be routinely bottled and that, plus the novelty of the color, gave them a cachet. Today, the style is fruity with just a hint of malt and a dry finish, an impression of light elegance.

- Eldridge Pope Royal Oak Pale Ale has a medium to full body and a sturdy bitterness.
- Sierra Nevada Pale Ale is fruity, with a lively bitterness and a light to medium body. Its signature citrus flavor comes from Cascade hops. It is also wonderfully fresh in most American markets.
- Bass Ale is the oldest beer brand in continuous operation, and their red triangle trademark is the earliest known registered mark. A thoroughly British outfit, their beer was brewed for a brief period in Latrobe, Pennsylvania.

Porter is a beer style characterized by a dark roasted flavor with a hint of sweetness. Porter was once a great deal more popular than it is now, as suggested by this letter dated 1 August, 1781:

> Sir: with Pleasure I do myself the Honor to acknowledge the Receipt of your Favor of 5th June last, with the two Cheese and Cask of Porter which accompanied it. Will you Sir, be pleased to do me the Favor to convey to the Commonwealth of Massa. Bay and to Capt. Sampson, my sincere and respectable thanks for this generous and very acceptable Present.

The letter is signed by a certain George Washington. In the years after independence and before he assumed the presidency, Washington was the customer of one Robert Hare, a porter brewer who had immigrated to Philadelphia in 1773. On July 20, 1788, a few days after the festivities commemorating the anniversary of the Declaration of Independence and Pennsylvania's ratification of the new Constitution, Washington wrote to his agent, Clement Biddle

> I beg you will send me a gross of Mr. Hairs best bottled

Porter if the price is not much enhanced by the copious draughts you took of it at the late Procession.

In 1789, on her way to join the president in New York, Martha Washington stopped in Philadelphia and entertained Hare and some other notables. The guests drank ten bottles of Madeira, one bottle of champagne, two bottles of claret, forty-five bowls of punch, ten bottles of American porter, one bottle of Taunton Ale and two bottles of crab cider.

By 1790, Washington was living in Federal Hall on Wall Street from whence his secretary wrote

> Will you be so good as to desire Mr Hare to have, if he continues to make the best Porter in Philadelphia, 3 gross of his best put up for Mt. Vernon? as the President means to visit that place in the recess of Congress and it is probable there will be a large demand for Porter at that time.

By 1796, Washington was leaving the presidency and retiring to Mt. Vernon. Hare's brewery had burned down and Washington was buying his porter from another brewery at the corner of Dock and Pear Streets. As with some other beer names that we've encountered, the name porter on a beer label can mean a lot of very different things.

- Young's Original London Porter is brewed by one of London's last independent brewers. Its age and location confer a certain legitimacy on its rendition of the style, which is medium-bodied with a mild hops aroma that is overshadowed by coffee and molasses notes. The head is beige and creamy. Serve at 45° to 50°F.
- Anchor Porter is decidedly sweet and very seductive. The sweetness supports a malty complexity that's barely balanced by a just detectable bitterness. This is a paradoxical beer, one

that can be rich and sustaining in cold weather and smooth and satisfying in the heat. Frequently seen on Ten Best Beers lists.

- Three Floyds Alpha Klaus Christmas Porter is a big, clunky porter that's not called a stout only because of its pronounced hoppiness. Chocolate-laden, rich and luscious.
- Yuengling Porter, brewed at the oldest brewery in America, is light and crisp with hints of roasted flavor. It's called porter even though it is a bottom-fermented lager beer, pleasant but not likely to resemble either the London original or other porters.

Roggen is a beer made with up to 50 percent rye. The flavor is grainy and tart with a clean finish and would be perfect with a pastrami sandwich.

- Goose Island Brewpub in Chicago makes a delicious bock version, which it releases as a spring seasonal.

Sahti is a traditional country beer of Finland. It is mostly home-brewed and made from a mixture of rye and barley. The mash is filtered through a mass of juniper branches and berries. During a guest stint as a brewer at a small craft brewery, I had the chance to brew and sample sahti. It was thoroughly likeable, light and refreshing, and the juniper character was strong. If you'd put an olive in the glass, it wouldn't have felt out of place.

Scotch ale and Scottish ale are the beers that made Scotland famous. Scotch ales are malt-laden, full-bodied and usually dark. (Malt was never taxed in Scotland, which may have encouraged its liberal use.) Many examples use some malt that has been kilned over a peat-smoke fire for a distinctive smoky nose. Scotch ales today generally avoid the use of imported hops and rely on heather and spruce and other seasonings. In some ways, Scotch ales are a testimony to the complexity of human nature. They have a sense of extraordinary decency and gentleness about them; goodness should be listed on the label with the rest of the ingredients. It's hard to believe that these are the drinks esteemed by guys who went off to battle in dresses. Serve at 50° to 55°F, the sweeter examples getting more of a chill.

- MacAndrews Scotch Ale has what may be one of the most charming labels in beerdom. The beer inside is dark, rich and surprisingly dry, with a roasted intensity that lingers on the palate.
- McEwan's Scotch Ale is one of the most thoroughly malty things I've ever tasted. A bottle would be in order if you weren't sure what part of the taste of beer comes from malt. It is only slightly sweet, but of such enormous body that it almost feels soapy in the mouth. It is also insanely inviting and comforting to drink. I recommend it for the common cold.
- And then there's Traquair House Ale. Somehow these people have taken malt, with its characteristic rich and simple bouquet, and turned it into a complex fruit, dark and mysterious. The length of the finish could be measured in hours. Traquair House is made in tiny batches in "the ancient brew house of the oldest inhabited house in Scotland." It is priced accordingly.

Scottish ales are like Scotch ales, but less so. They have lower gravities, and therefore less alcohol and less unfermented sugar and body. They are closer in spirit to English ales.
- Grant's Scottish ale is made in Yakima, Washington. It has less in common with the other Scotch ales and more with British bitters. Grant's is more hopped than the rest with only tiny hints of roasted flavor. It is thoroughly refreshing.
- Kiltlifter ale is just slightly sweet. The sweetness supports a complexity of other malty flavors and aromas. A slightly chilled bottle of Kiltlifter Scottish ale can cure winter. To the American palate, this is very big beer; in Scotland it's a lite.

Stout sounds serious doesn't it? Stout-hearted men and all that. According to the recipes I've seen, stout and porter are pretty much the same product except that stout substitutes a small amount of flaked barley and an increased amount of roasted barley for some of the malt in porter. Both styles rely on Fuggles and Kent Goldings hops for their bitterness, and both use no aroma hops. The two styles are historically related too. After porter became popular in London in the 1730s, a richer, more alcoholic version called extra stout porter was introduced.

The most famous stout is the one brewed by the Irish firm of Arthur Guinness. It has a loyal following in Ireland and among Irish émigrés in every country except this one. There are several different versions of Guinness Stout: a domestic draft and bottled, an export bottle, a special tropical, high-gravity bottled version and now something called Pub Draft Guinness in a can with a special gas-producing insert that mimics the creamy head of a nitrogen-based pub draft system,

There are other Irish stouts. You can find the softer and more approachable Murphy's at the Oyster Bar at the Plaza Hotel in New York. There are also English stouts which tend to sweetness and are more charming than provocative.

In the Caribbean, Guinness ("Guinness for Power") and Courage ("Take Courage") are endowed with a curious mix of magical powers. Small amounts are said to be good for pregnant women and babies; large amounts are thought to improve men's sexual desire and performance.

Serve stout as warm as you dare. In general, as you learn to like this style, you'll prefer it warmer, up to a maximum of about 60°F.

- Mackeson XXX Stout is a sweet and unbelievably silky beer with a modest beige head and a long iced mocha coffee finish with just a touch of roasted flavor.
- Anderson Valley Barley Flats Oatmeal Stout from Boonville, California, is a major American entry into the category. Its taste

is simpler and more direct than the European stouts, without resorting to high alcohol levels. This stout contains both oats and wheat along with barley malt and enough roasted barley to make a lovely brown head. It's opaque, and I for one have to admire any beer you can't see through. My guess is that this is a beer that's perfectly formulated for the American market and (if the price were a bit more competitive) has a chance to catch on as a cult favorite.

- Old Australia Stout from the South Australia Brewing Company is pleasant and off-dry. A good introduction to stout and the other sweeter, maltier beers.
- St. Ambroise Oatmeal Stout from McAuslan Brewing Company in Montreal has a short-lived brown head, opaque iced-coffee color and a bitter, malted milk and cappucino flavor built on a light to medium body.
- Dogfish Head's Worldwide Stout is so purely malty and roasty that it could be an archetype: a great beer to have at a tasting for its maximum focus on malt.

Thomas Hardy's Ale is another brand that's become a style. It is brewed by Eldridge Pope in Dorchester, England. It tastes like a whisky-soaked caramel candy and is almost as chewy. It weighs in at 10% alcohol, is bottle aged and vintage dated. It carries the following statement on the label:

> In 'The Trumpet Major' Hardy wrote of Dorchester's famous ale "It was of the most beautiful color that the eye of an artist in beer could desire; full in body, yet brisk as a volcano; piquant yet without a twang, luminous as an autumn sunset."

Compare those lines, if you will, with the immortal:
LESS FILLING! TASTES GREAT!

In spite of being a beer that seems to have opted for the virtues of its stronger cousins, Thomas Hardy's is not at all freakish. If you find a bottle, try to find a friend or two to share it with in the later part of the evening. You may find that the best aspects of its taste are better done in other drinks: you might find yourself thinking of a glass of Madeira. But the thought of the tiny hand-crafted production may keep you interested.

Trappist hearkens back to the time when every monastery above the grape-growing latitudes made its own beer. It was the safest beverage for the monks, of course, but it was also necessary to monastic hospitality. In Charlemagne's time, the monastery of St. Gall had two brew houses, one for guests and another for the community itself. At about the same time, the regulations of the Abbey of St. Denis, among others, had written instructions for the furnishing of breweries and the brewing of beer, which they called cervisia.

All these beers are top-fermented ales and bottle conditioned, and most of them are worth keeping silent for. (Trappist monks are noted for their vow of silence.) Their flavors differ, but they all have substantial body and lingering finishes. Abbey beers are commercially made in a similar style. Trappist Ales typically are produced in three strengths. There are no bad examples, but you are most likely to find:

- Chimay (Red Label) is sedimented and bottle conditioned. It comes in a 750ml (25 oz.) bottle with a champagne-like cork and wire basket. It's dark copper colored, with an almost white head and medium body. It has a wine-like bouquet and a tart, refreshing first impression on the palate, followed by an almost pillowy softness. Delicious at any temperature, Chimay is preferred by devotees at 50° to 60°F. The date of bottling is stamped on the cork, and a year or two of bottle age is considered an asset.

The Blue Label is a more assertive version of the red and there

is a white label that is crisp and dry and very "accessible" to American beer explorers.
- Orval is the most perfectly dry Trappist beer. The flavor has changed over the years, but the distinctive, alluring bitterness remains. Orval is on a lot of Ten Best Lists.

Wee heavy is the Scots' way to order the very heaviest and darkest Scotch Ale. The heavy in question is "wee" because the bottle size is smaller than a regular ale. The bottle is smaller because the ale is bigger.

Wheat beers take advantage of the fact that, with some difficulty, wheat can be malted and mashed just like barley, and the sweet result can be fermented into both ale and lager. The taste that wheat gives to beer is considerably different from barley's, but wheat is far from being a mere economical adjunct. A portion of wheat added to a barley mash creates a beer with lighter body, a noticeably refreshing tang and excellent head retention. The sharpness shows best at a serving temperature of 48° to 50°F.

The amount of wheat in a recipe can vary from as little as 10 percent to as high as 60 percent, and the wheat may be malted or added in the form of raw flakes.

There are three traditional ales that use a considerable portion of wheat:
- Witbier or bière blanche is the traditional white beer of Belgium.
- Hoegaarden is the beer without which there would be no summer. It is both crisp and soft on the palate with a beguiling citrus/yeast character. Pronounced who-garden and often called for at the bar as simply "the Who." A product of Anheuser-Busch InBev, the world's largest brewing company, the Who proves that big guys can do it right.
- Saison Dupont: see both Summer Beer and Farmhouse Ale.

Weizen, the spicy, golden, clove-like beer of Bavaria. The modifier *hefe-* (German: yeast) means that the beer is unfiltered and that the cloudiness you see is from yeast and the protein in the wheat.

- Julius Echter Hefe-Weissbier is remarkably rich with subtle spicy notes: a wine-lover's beer.
- Berliner Weisse, the eccentric, sour, lactic drink of Berlin, gets its peculiar flavor from a special yeast. It is served in a fishbowl-like goblet with a generous splash of raspberry syrup. People who have had the good fortune to drink Berliner Weisse in Germany tell me that the unadorned version is crisp and noble and that the fruited one is a waste of good talent. My experience with an example imported into this country has been quite the opposite.

Almost every brewpub and microbrewery will be making a wheat beer in the summer months, and some of those beers will be held year-round.

Lagers

Bock is a very strong, slightly sweet and usually dark Beer Style originally brewed in the German town of Einbeck. The original Bocks were brewed in the winter, stored in the cold and drunk in the spring. There are several stories about what the word itself means, but for us moderns, "bock" means "more": more color, more sweetness, more flavor, more alcohol. There is even, saints preserve us, an intensified bock called Doppelbock. Yes, doppel means exactly what you think it means (See below). Since no good deed ever goes unexaggerated, there are now Triple Bocks whose alcohol levels are well up into double digits.

There are also several stories about how bock is made. Some of the stories are absurd, all are fantasies. Bock gets to be what it is by having more malt and darker malt at the beginning and more alcohol and unfermented sugar at the end.

- Schneider Aventinus is a summery bock made with a portion of wheat. It is both substantial and refreshing and would be—in its draft version at least—on most Ten Best Beers in the World lists.

Clear beer/alcopop/malternatives in their current form can't really call themselves beer at all. Instead they are "malt beverages," meaning that they get some small portion of their alcohol from malt. Three points here:

- Is clear beer a good idea in itself? Well, who knows? At the least, any answers to the question are premature. Maybe this micro-filtered drink will serve as the basis for the drinks that stir the souls, or at least the tastebuds, of our great grandchildren.
- Of course, the rising voices of The Beer Nation will all be raised against it. That's all right; beer drinkers, and beer lovers particularly, tend to conserve rather than innovate. Note the slow acceptance of hops—the city of London once had a law forbidding its use—and lagering, which was reviled in America as a foreign and over-delicate innovation. The microbrews and brewpubs that I dote on are facing the same kind of resistance.
- If you want to explore the matter, the only thing to do is to taste some of the stuff in privacy and form your own opinion. I once had a taste of a product from Coors called Zima (pronounced ZEE-ma). The flavor recalled Perrier water and gin and tonic with a twist. The product was euthanized recently.

There are some other questions worthy of your attention.

- How is clear beer being marketed? I know that a beverage shouldn't be judged by its sales force, but there's something fishy about the way clear beer is being presented to the public, something that makes me think that the spirit behind the product is not entirely an ethically hedonistic one. The bottle (and indeed the color and taste of the product itself) seems to suggest the bottled waters that are all the rage. Beer isn't water, and the difference should be celebrated, not disguised. There is also something childish about the colors and the labeling, something that makes me wonder if they're targeting a young consumer; maybe even an underage consumer.

- What is behind the sudden passion for clarity? In the nineties we saw clear gasoline, clear soaps, clear mouthwashes and clear soft drinks. All of these products are marketed without the slightest suggestion that clarity affects the taste or performance of the products themselves. Maybe it's nothing more than evidence of fashion's insatiable appetite for the new. (It's New! It's Clear!) Perhaps it's an indication of a longer-cycle change, one that takes us further from the natural roots of things and deeper into a celebration of our own manufacturing. In any case, maintain vigilance; keep your clears straight—don't rinse after meals with the gasoline or mix rum and a slice of lime with the detergent.

To confess my own conservatism, I don't have much hope for clear beer except as an alcohol-delivery system for folks who may be too young to drink anyway. At the moment, it's a drink made from malt that is trying to suppress its connection with its own ingredients. I can't think of a single innovation, culinary or otherwise, that made a contribution based on a throttled connection with its source.

Doppelbock is Bock but more so. It is an even richer, darker, sweeter and more alcoholic brew than Bock. Doppelbock originated in Munich. The original was a monastic brew called Salvator, produced by the brothers of St. Francis of Paula and first sold to the public in 1780. All the brands of doppelbock are easy to recognize because they express their kinship to the original in the suffix -ator. Serve them lightly chilled.

- Kulminator or E.K.U. 28, is the beer that every bartender used to identify as the world's strongest. The 28 refers to the original specific gravity as measured in the European system (degrees Plato). Kulminator's high alcohol dominates the flavor of the beer; there is also a pronounced syrupy component and no discernible hop aroma.

- Paulaner Salvator often shows up in this country roughly handled. At its best, there is a malty complexity coupled with full body and roundness of character that's a delight. More frequently, it's sweet and dead. Buy from a careful retailer.
- Celebrator is relatively light for a doppelbock, with a mildly spicy flavor.

Dortmunder is a lager beer style from Dortmund, Germany's largest brewing center. Less bitter than a pilsner and less malty than a Munich, the most famous example (and the one most widely available in the US) is DAB.

Dry beer is light beer's first cousin; another beer without a finish. Since so much of what makes beer wonderful is missing in dry beer, it's not surprising that the dry beer business is drying up.

One place where dry beer has been successful is in Japan, where the quickly disappearing taste goes well with delicately flavored, slightly sour or salty foods.

Eisbock is a variation of the Bock style that is made even stronger by a kind of primitive distillation. Bock beer is chilled until some ice forms. The ice, which is almost entirely water, is removed and the resulting stronger beer is bottled.

- Kulminator, one of the strongest beers in the world at 10.6% by weight, is made by this method, which is formally known as congelation.
- Hakusekikan produces a 28% ABV version that manages not to be overwhelmed by its alcohol.

Heineken forces us to ask: Can a brand be a style? Heineken is the third largest brewer in the world, behind SAB Miller and Imbed (Budweiser), and the world's largest exporter of beer. Heineken and Amstel combine to make Holland the largest single supplier of imported beer to the US (23 percent of the total import volume is Heineken). In the Caribbean and other parts of tropical America, a "green" is still the substitute for uncertain drinking water. Heineken is light-bodied Euro-pils with a citrusy tang. In its first days in the American market, it won a lot of fans simply by contrast with the domestic competition.

Keller is an unfiltered beer style based on German Pils. It has a bit more thickness in the mouth than most German beers.
• New Glarus Brewing produces a tart version at about 4% that has an arresting creamy texture with a tartness that resembles white wine.

Lawnmower beer is a slightly affectionate, slightly disparaging name used by beer cognoscenti to describe those beers whose outstanding virtue is their wetness. The image is of a fellow who has just humped a snarling, bucking mower mulched monster through .352 acres of Kentucky bluegrass and is settling back to see what he has wrought and reward himself with a frosty cold one.

Ironically, the pleasure of cold beer after hot work has come to be recognized by serious brewers as something worthy of their consideration, and this author has served as a judge at Philadelphia's Annual Chili and Lawnmower Beer Competition.

Light beer, in spite of what you might think, was not invented by our generation. Brewers have always been interested in using less malt to get more beer. A first step was made in 1817 with the introduction of Patent Malt, a barley malt that gave a reassuringly dark color to ale even when used in tiny amounts. It was the beginning of the relatively light stouts and porters.

What porter did in the UK, lager did in the US. Clearer beers that were less burdened with flavor required less malt to produce and were automatically lighter. As mass marketing and price competition changed the developing American Pilsner Style, it became lighter in flavor and alcohol.

Tax systems have always taxed strong beers more vigorously than mild ones, giving the lighter beers the advantage of price in the market place. In our country and the UK, fermentable cereals were rationed during World War I and their use in beer restricted.

It was only a few decades ago that someone thought of addressing the problem of calories. The first effort was called Gablinger's and it was advertised as "diet beer." I remember it as pretty good stuff, hoppy and ahead of its time. It failed miserably, perhaps because it reminded beer drinkers of dieting every time they picked one up.

These days, light beer is more cleverly marketed. "Filling" is a wonderful code word for fattening. It lets the advertiser make a patently ridiculous claim without being thought a knave, and it lets us believe him without thinking of ourselves as fools.

The actual trick of making light beer is this: you start out with a wort that is about 15 percent less concentrated than regular beer. Then you add an enzyme called amyloglucoside. AMG converts all the complex, non-fermentable sugars into simple fermentable ones. The simple sugars are then converted to alcohol by the yeast. The resulting beer has about the same amount of alcohol as "heavy" beer but none of the dextrins that make for full body. Of course it's less filling; the lingering finish that ennobles so many wonderful beers has disappeared.

Now, at the heart of all this light beer business is a ridiculous fantasy. It's the childish notion that you can eat and drink and stay slim, as if the laws of the universe will stop just for you. Maybe you can even smoke and still breathe, spend and not go into debt, cad about and still have a finely wrought and treasureable love.

Maybe you can, but at least as far as the beer is concerned, the hidden price of the deal is that you give up the taste of the thing. Eventually you even forget that there was a taste to surrender. Hooray for you, slim! How about a nice cold Mephistopheles Lite?

Malt liquor used to be almost a synonym for beer. In a letter to Thomas Jefferson, Joseph Coppinger insisted that a national brewery would "improve the quality of the malt liquors in every point of the Union." A revenue bill in 1866 included malt liquor in the larger category of beer. A Supreme Court opinion, Sarils v. United States, recognized that malt liquor was an essentially beer-like product of fermentation, not a spiritous outcome of distillation. Tax laws referred to malt liquor as a cousin of beer, ale and porter right up until Prohibition in 1919. One Prohibition-era law, in 1927, referred to malt liquor as being different from beer by virtue of a higher alcohol content.

After repeal, the Internal Revenue Code of 1939 referred to "fermented malt liquors," "fermented liquors" and "malt liquors" when speaking of beer. Returning to an earlier sense of the word, it used these terms in distinction to distilled spirits. By 1954, the general term had again become beer.

The product that is marketed as malt liquor in the United States today is more like whisky with a screw top than beer, even though no distillation is involved. This malt liquor is fortified with sugar before fermentation to increase the amount of alcohol in the finished product. Michael Jackson, the pioneering English beer writer, cites the first of the species as Stite Malt Liquor, produced in Minneapolis in 1942. At as much as 8 percent alcohol, (compared to about 3.5–5 percent for most beers) a single 40 oz. dose of malt liquor has greater intoxicating effect than a six-pack of common beer. It is also considerably cheaper, takes less time to drink and occupies a lot less belly space, so the drunk get drunker faster.

Maerzen is a German lager, traditionally brewed in March and made stronger than average table beers to survive aging in cellars and caves until it was served in the fall. In Bavaria, Maerzenbier became associated with Oktoberfest. Maerzens are malty, pale and have about 4.5 percent alcohol.

Munich is the city where lager brewing began, so it's not surprising that it has given its name to a family of beer styles. The paler style, called Helles, is a medium coppery-brown. The darker version of the Munich style, called Dunkel, is a real surprise for most Americans and British. Its warm, dark brown color suggests a stout or at least a dark ale. In fact, it and the Helles are both smooth, malty lagers, lightly hopped, scarcely bitter and very full bodied.

Serve Munich beers at just under 50°F.

• Spaten (in both pale and dark versions) is the only example of Munich style beers that is widely available in America. Both these beers have generous mouth feel and malty bouquet. The light version is particularly impressive.

Oktoberfest is a beer festival held every year in Munich for sixteen days from late September to early October. By extension, packaged beers done in this malty rich lager style.

• Ayinger Oktober Fest-Maerzen is a soft middle-weight with a coffeeish flavor and a distinct aroma of Hallertau hops. It is somewhat dry for the style.

Partial Malt Beers. There are some delicious beers made with something other than barley malt providing the grist, but most partial malt beers are mere creatures of economy. Barley malt is expensive; rice and corn sugar are not. With a few Scandinavian exceptions, most partial malt beers are designed to appeal to the consumer who wants the most alcohol for the buck. Many of today's beer lovers started out drinking these beers and then had an "aha" moment when they tasted something slightly better.

Many of the people reading this book will recognize a period in their lives when they drank something with even less malt character. These were the cheap beers of college. They got to be so cheap because they are brewed by adding large amounts of corn and rice to a small amount of malted barley and are made with industrial care and in industrial quantities. They were cold, passed under the threshold of your gag reflex, and had enough alcohol to pass the time. They are still around.

If you've tried one or two beers from each category in the pilsner (see below) style, and paid attention to the tastes, you've probably been surprised at the range of tastes. These beers are related, but they probably seem like distant cousins. Since pilsner is the beer style that most Americans grew up with, it's probably a good place to start exploring the taste of beer. Be sure to find a bar that serves a lot of good beer and serves it at the right temperature. For pilsner, that temperature is between 45° and 50°F, with the better beers begging for the higher end of the scale.

Pilsner is a light-to-medium-bodied, highly carbonated beer style with a pronounced hops bouquet. Pilsner is made from the palest of malts and uses large amounts of Saaz and Hallertau hops for bitterness and aroma. A relative newcomer, it is the bottom-fermented or lager beer style imitated by most of our mass-market brands. The name comes from the town of Pilsn in Czechoslovakia. (In German the –er suffix attached to a place name means something from that place.) Can you guess what they call the pilsner-style beer from the nearby town of Budweis?

Real Pilsner

If you would like to taste the original pilsner that everyone has copied, order Pilsner Urquell. Urquell means original, and this is the beer from Pilsn that started it all. Urquell (as it's usually known) is actually made with a top-fermenting yeast and has a generous malty profile. To many tasters, it's the most ale-like of all the lagers. You can also try to get the original beer from Budweis in the Czech Republic. This is the beer that's known as Budweiser in Europe. In the US there was a bit of a trade dispute over who owned the right to the name. Did it belong to the giant Anheuser-Busch (now owned by the even larger InBev) or to the tiny brewery in Budejovický in the Czech Republic? To the surprise of many, the American court's decision went in favor of A-B. If you're in an American bar and want to taste the beer from Budweis, you'll have to ask for Czechvar.

In America, the best pilsners are:

• the muscular and malty Tuppers Hop Pocket
• the bready, low-alcohol, perfectly hopped Pennsylvania Kaiser Pils and
• the smooth and herbal Prima Pils

With these Pilsners, freshness is everything. Try to taste them in a place that sells a lot and turns over its supply quickly.

Europils

Beers that aren't from Pilsn can't be called Pilsner and are known by the diminutive "pils." Compared to the Urquell ilk, they are a lot less statuesque. Most European brewers don't have brewing water that can take a large charge of hops without the beer becoming unpleasantly bitter. These wannabees are therefore much lighter in hops aroma and so are less malty, even though they are made entirely from real malt. They do have the same carbonation and alcohol levels. Beck's, St. Pauli Girl and DAB are examples made entirely from malt. They are excellent beers, clean and refreshing and mild-flavored.

American Pilsner

This is a medium-alcohol, timidly flavored style of beer that emerged after Prohibition as first the cheapest and then the dominant form of American beer. The lack of character may explain why Americans, many from strong beer-drinking roots, drink less beer per capita than a dozen other countries, including wine-loving countries like Spain and Austria.

The American style arose after Prohibition when it must have seemed like a clean, refreshing alternative to the murky, badly made, illegal beers of the twenties. When the Noble Experiment ended, all the eccentric local breweries had been destroyed. Their beers were replaced by national brands whose strength was their advertising, not their flavor. Instead of lots of local beers brewed to delight a small audience, we had a few national brands designed to avoid offending a large one. Pilsner is king in the rest of the world's beer market too, but in America it rules alone.

Canadians make a slightly heartier product in the same spirit. Moosehead is the most robust, but Labatt and Molson also brew a clean and flavorful product.

The three main brewers of American Pilsner—Budweiser, Miller and Coors—have all been purchased by foreign brewing conglomerates, and it will be interesting to see how the beers change in response to new ownership and shifting tastes. (See Partial Malt Beers, above)

Discussion Questions
1. With all this variety, does the idea of having a "favorite" beer seem a bit odd?
2. If a bottle of beer only says "premium" on the label, what does that mean about the beer?
3. Did reading about any of these styles make your mouth water?
4. Would you spend the night at a convent that didn't brew a good beer for its guests?
5. What's the best Dopplebock name you can come up with? Gladiator is already taken.

6. Which do you think is the best strategy for developing a good beer palate: tasting one of each of these styles until you've done the whole list or tasting one style quite a few times in a row?

Monk's Cafe in Philadelphia.

Chapter 8

Who Makes Beer?

When you finish this chapter, you will
• know the major players in the beer industry
• have some idea of why your beer costs what it does
• have an idea of how much of your beer dollar is spent on ads

Industrial Brewers

TOTAL US BEER INDUSTRY, MAJOR
BREWERS & IMPORTERS
Information Provided by Beer Marketer's Insights 2006

Company	Shipments (000 bbls)	Market share (%)
AB	103,025	48.5
Miller	38,050	18.3
Coors	23,250	10.9
Heineken USA	8,502	3.6
Pabst	6,500	3.3
Gambrinus	6,416	2.9
Barton	5,807	2.5
InBev	3,580	1.9
Guinness	3,288	1.6
Boston	1,580	0.6
Yuengling	1,580	0.7
Other	12,600	5.4
Total	214,178	

This list looks quite a bit different from the list of top producers published by the Brewers Institute in 1991. Back then, the biggest six brewers accounted for 96 percent of the beer sold. All im-

ports had about a 4 percent share of the market and craft beers were around 1.5 percent.

The Three Tier System:

When Prohibition was repealed in 1933, states were given the power to regulate sales of alcohol within their borders. One result was radical prohibition of cross-ownership or control: companies that produced wine, beer or spirits were not allowed to sell their products at retail. They weren't even allowed to sell directly to retailers.

The thinking at the time was that vertical integration of the industry would lead to aggressive promotion of alcohol, and thus to excessive consumption. This Three Tier System, which was supposed to weaken the grip of saloons on their customers, instead created a class of wholesale distributors with their own lobbying organizations. Today, the system is attacked for restricting the ability of small breweries to find a wholesaler and therefore to reach the public. The Three Tier System is supported by the highly lucrative wholesale segment of the industry and promoted as an effective way to tax and control sales.

Microbreweries/Craft Breweries.

A microbrewery is any brewery whose annual production is less than 15,000 barrels. In 1991, there were 88 microbreweries in the US, ten of which opened in that year. Fifteen thousand thirty-one gallon barrels may not sound very micro to you, amounting as it does to 200,000 cases of beer. In the world of megabreweries, however, this is small beer indeed. Anheuser-Busch makes this much beer every ninety minutes or so, and Coors makes about that much on a single shift.

A craft brewery is one whose emphasis is on producing rich tasting, interesting beers whose price may often be higher than that of beers produced with an emphasis on bland taste and low price.

In 1991, all micro/craft breweries accounted for 400,000 barrels (bbls), which is less than 0.25 percent of all the beer consumed in the country. In 2007, craft beer sales of 6,000,000 bbls were 3.8 percent by volume and 5.9 percent by dollars. Small as they are, micros are increasing their volume in the US at the rate of 12 percent annually and their sales at 16 percent, at a time when total beer sales are scarcely growing at all. In Canada the 150,000-barrel production is growing at an annual rate of 20 percent.

Microbrewed beers are usually of much higher quality than industrial beers and this is reflected in their price. If a volume of Budweiser at the beer wholesaler's shop costs a dollar, an equal volume of Anchor Steam, purchased from the same source, will cost $1.69.

The boiling kettles at the Budvar brewery in the Czech Republic.

Why are these little breweries doing so well and why should you care? They are prospering because they are making small amounts of a carefully made product that is locally distributed to people who are willing to pay a bit more for superior quality. You care because the more of them there are, the better our beer is going to get. If they do well enough, they might even spur some of the giants to improve their product. For a discussion of the strategies that make a micro-brewery successful, see the book *Brewing up a Business* by Dogfish Head Brewery's Sam Calagione.

Contract Brewers.

Let's say you and a few of your friends decide to drop out of the fast-paced, hectic life of accountancy, shopping mall management and chiropody and open a tavern. You want the tavern to appeal to cool, beer-loving guys like yourselves, so you decide to brew your very own beer. Based on an inspiration, you decide to call it Three Guys Named Fred Lager.

Opening even a tiny brewery costs a lot of money, so you decide to have a commercial brewer make the beer for you. This beer is called a contract brew. Broadly speaking, there are four ways that your beer can be brewed. In descending order of expense:

1. A recipe can be formulated especially for your tastes, and individual batches brewed according to the recipe.
2. One of the brewer's regular products can be modified slightly by the addition of a specialty malt or some extra hops, and batches brewed as you order and as they fit in to the brewery's schedule.
3. Two or more of the brewer's existing beers can be blended together to make a "new" beer.
4. Some bottles of an already existing beer can be relabeled with the cool Three Guys Named Fred label. You should not be surprised if the very same beer turns up in a rival pub across town sporting their label.

The practice of contract brewing is perfectly respectable. At the top end of the list, it makes it possible for an entrepreneur with a vision to create some very special beer and devote her energy to selling it. If the entrepreneur has that vision at a time when there's a lot of excess brewing capacity around, so much the better.

The well-known Samuel Adams beers were contract brewed in the early days. Maureen Ogle observed wisely that "(Jim) Koch reduced his startup costs by hundreds of thousands of dollars and eliminated the two bugaboos that felled so many microbrewers: bad equipment and undercapitalization." Some of the other commendable contract brewed beers are: Brooklyn Brown Ale and Lager, Old Peconic Hampton Ale, Helenboch, Stone Mountain, Penn Pilsner (bottles), New Amsterdam, Olde Heurich and the resurrected Prior Double Dark.

When the purpose is solely commercial, and tasteless beer is re-labeled for merchandising purposes, the result is called private label beer. Sleazy examples of recent memory include Billy Beer and Nude Beer.

Interestingly, private beer labels in supermarkets have not done very well, even though they were much cheaper than the same beers in different cans with recognizable brand names. Beer isn't the only product to flop when it's repackaged as a house brand or generic. Other products you can't give away in the low-priced package: toothpaste, tuna fish and baby food.

Independents

In the beer trade, independents occupy a niche in between the big industrial conglomerates and the small craft brewers. They are regional companies that can afford to advertise and promote like the big boys. Independent breweries are making a comeback these days, partly on the strength of contract brewing.

There is only one independent—Yuengling—on the list of the ten biggest beer providers.

Brewpubs

A restaurant that brews beer and sells it for on-premises consumption is a brewpub. Brewpubs serve the freshest possible beer. Since transportation is a large part of the cost of beer, the beer they serve ought to be a bargain as well. At this writing, there are some 285 brewpubs in the United States. Some brewpubs are extensions of microbreweries which bottle or keg some of their beer to be sold elsewhere.

Brewpubs—even the few that have multiple outlets—have developed a warm fuzzy image that's often coupled with a genuine community involvement. You are likely to find your local brewpub involved with community agriculture and neighborhood organizations. They are often very kid-friendly places where you are more likely to see families with strollers than in any other taverns.

Atmospherics aside, brewpubs in urban areas often struggle with the economics of space. It takes a lot of room to properly store beer until it's ready to bottle or serve. If the space in question is expensive urban real estate, there's a temptation to either push the beer out when it's still a bit green, or to pick recipes based on the amount of time they need in the conditioning tanks. In general, the best brewpubs flourish where the rents are low or where the laws allow them to serve beers not made on the premises along with their own product.

Where is the brewpub nearest you? That's hard to say. In North America they are opening at the rate of one a week. (Their two-year survival rate is 75 percent, which is considered pretty good in the restaurant business, especially if you consider the extra cost of outfitting both a brewery and a restaurant.) If you want to know where the good beer is on your travels or in your neighborhood, you can consult one of the brewpub resources at:
http://www.shortcourseinbeer.com

Beer Bars

A few years ago, the very idea of calling a tavern a "beer bar" would have been incomprehensible. Of course there's beer—it's a bar! These days, when someone talks about a beer bar, they mean a place whose reputation is built, at least in part, on a wide selection of beer on tap and a respectable listing of bottles. You should be wary of advertising that stresses the number of different beers available. If there are "over 1000 beers!" on the menu, chances are that a lot of them will be outdated and stale.

Some beer bars are legendary. The aforementioned Monk's Cafe in Philadelphia, the Brickskellar in Washington, the recently-opened Spuyten Duyvel in Brooklyn, Baltimore's Max's on Broadway, The Toronado in San Francisco and the Beer Bistro in Toronto come to mind as North American pilgrimage sites.

Working at the brewery. Photo courtesy of Matt Wiater

A barrel, by the way, is the standard measure of beer production. The US barrel is equal to thirty-one gallons. Barrel is abbreviated bbl, which sounds like bubble and therefore looks just about right. A barrel is what they call a "notional measurement." It means that there aren't any actual thirty-one-gallon barrels, it's simply a way to say how much beer is out and about.

So don't expect to see any bbls in the cooler at your neighborhood tavern. Those large cylindrical things are called kegs and they hold half a barrel or 15.5 gallons. To confuse matters a bit, they are sometimes called "halves" or half-kegs. There is a smaller cylinder that's half the size of a keg and is therefore sometimes called a "quarter." Some high-quality specialty beers come in high-priced specialty sizes.

The fifteen-and-a-half-gallon keg contains a minimum of 165 twelve-ounce beer glasses. Allowing for the space in the glass taken up by the head, 180 to 190 glasses is probably the norm.

Where Does My Money Go?

Prices

Beer is cheap. Anybody can afford it. In spite of this, many people scrutinize the price of beer more than they do the price of other foods.

So what determines the price of beer? Whaddya think? Of course it has something to do with supply and demand, and demand has a great deal to do with quality. Turned around, that means that in general, you get what you pay for and that price reflects value. There are three factors that make this so.

The first is scarcity. There is a limit to how much beer can be brewed in the smallest, most quality-conscious breweries, and that limit is not very flexible. It's hard to double your production of Blue Dog Ale just because you got discovered and demand went up.

Another thing that makes good beer expensive is the cost of labor. Smaller breweries usually have a higher labor cost per unit of beer; they don't call it craft-brewed for nothing.

An astonishingly high proportion of the cost of beer is the cost of the containers. Of the total cost of a pallet of canned industrial beer at the brewery loading dock, 69 percent is the cost of the can. As we saw earlier, lower packaging costs per unit of volume make draft beer considerably cheaper than bottled or canned.

The last factor is transportation. Good beer is made all over the world, and if you call for a beer that comes from far away, you have to pay its cab fare.

Really good beers are usually lightly advertised. That cost, which is such a large part of the cost of industrial brews, doesn't add much to the price of better beer.

It's helpful, when you consider the price of beer, to remember two aphorisms that are very useful because they're mostly true.

"You pay for what you get."

"You get what you pay for."

The whole truth and the good news is something like this: "You get what you pay for, except when you don't." The market is not perfect. There are a lot of other things that create demand besides quality. Just as there are beers that are overpriced because the prestige attached to their names has increased the demand for them beyond what their quality would dictate, there are beers whose relative obscurity masks a very high quality. Sometimes a local beer, by virtue of its freshness, is the best value around, regardless of its price. It's possible to find and enjoy these glitches in the usual market relationship. In fact, there's a certain heady pleasure in it.

Finally, it's important to keep the question of price in context. Purchased by the case, almost all of the best beers in the world cost less than $3 for a 12 oz. bottle. (That's a figure based on the tax-crazed Northeast of the US.) I can think of only a handful of beers, hand-crafted, bottle-fermented ones, that cost close to $4.

Take that three bucks out into the world of delicious things and see what it gets you: one-third of a bottle of good simple table wine, a cup of exotic coffee, half a half a dozen cherrystone clams. One of the beautiful things about beer is how inexpensively it lets you get in touch with exquisitely delicious things.

In 1976, for every dollar's worth of beer shipped from a brewery, sixty-one cents had been spent on materials. By 1987, only forty-six cents' worth of goods went into a buck's worth of beer.

Beer has resisted the allure of veblenizing—at least so far. Veblenizing is the process by which things become valued for their high price alone. In the world of drinks, veblenizing has led to $2,500 bottles of Cabernet and $600 for a hand-blown bottle filled with 500ml of grappa. Craft beer, on the other hand, has steadfastly resisted becoming Designer Beer.

Part of the reason may lie in beer's humble raw materials: there's almost nothing cheaper and more thoroughly commoditized than barley. Hops can occasionally be pricey, but they are used in small amounts and price spikes are usually quickly cancelled by new plantings. Just as important is the notion that the culture of beer loving emerged in the context of values that emerged in the 1970s, values that stressed experience and devalued status. Beer lovers seem to be willing to pay more for great beer, but they don't seem especially anxious for the world to know how expensive it is.

Retail.

Americans spend about $97 billion a year on beer. That's in the neighborhood of six and a half dollars a person a week, or about what it costs to buy the Philadelphia Inquirer every day of the week. It's about half of what it costs to have cable TV and a twentieth of the cost of private health insurance for a family of three. A month's worth of beer is about the same price as a tank of gas for a medium-sized car.

That $97 billion compares to about $24 billion spent on movies from the major studios.

Imports.

Imported beer represents about 8 percent of the market, in spite of a tremendous price disadvantage.

Taxes.

On January 1 of 1991, Federal excise tax on beer was doubled to $18.00 a barrel. That comes to about six cents for every twelve-ounce glass, can or bottle. That same year, beer sales in America slipped by about 2 percent. (You may remember the headlines— Beer Bubble Bursts; Excise Tax Hops on Beer Industry Growth; Beer Sales Flat; and so on.)

There are state excise taxes too. They range from Alabama's ambitious $32.65 a barrel to Wyoming's afterthoughtish $0.62. The 1991 average state tax was $7.32. Beer is also subject to local taxes, sales taxes and gross receipt taxes. The brewing industry likes to talk about the disastrous effect of taxes on beer sales and jobs and the economy. You can look forward to industry spokespersons citing the 1991 coincidence as evidence of cause and effect. Industry analysts claim that 44 percent of the costs of a serving of beer are tax associated. The excise tax on beer began during the Civil War as a temporary measure.

There are other taxes on beer: general sales taxes, special alcohol sales taxes, and even special taxes for on-premise consumption of alcohol, not to mention special alcohol sales taxes and other levies in many major tourist cities.

Tied House

In nineteenth century America and contemporary England, a tavern tied to a particular brewery by mortgage holding or outright ownership. Tied houses serve only the products of the owning brewery and have been blamed in England for stifling competition and killing off traditional ales. Tied houses, and indeed most vertical business relationships in the beer industry, are forbidden by law in the US. Before Prohibition, local breweries had used tied houses to shut the large national brewers out of their markets, so after Repeal, the large brewers drafted and lobbied for the legislation that made tied houses illegal. While they were doing that, they also worked for regulations that liberalized off-premise sales of bottles and cans of beer. Tied houses decreased the variety of beer available.

Value of Shipments

Beer is very conspicuous in American life. It has its own billboards, its signs are neon. Its tee shirts cover chests and bellies and its logos are stamped on just about every public spectacle. I found myself wondering if it takes up as much space in the economy as it does in the popular imagination. One way to look at the subject would be to compare the amount of money people spend on beer with the amount they spend on other things. This turns out to be less direct a measure than you might think. Retail sales are tracked by industry groups, and not all of the information is public. Some figures are good guesses, others no more than bragging or wishful thinking.

The folks who do keep track of these things are the good people at the Department of Commerce, particularly the Bureau of the Census. What they measure is the price paid for goods as they leave America's factories. The measure is referred to as "value of shipments." The value of all industry shipments of malt beverages was $15.9 billion in 1991. If a billion of anything is as unreal to you as it is to me, it might help to know that beer shipments are about the same in value as:

- all the commercially made bread, cakes and related products, which, considering the close family ties between bread and beer, seems fitting
- all the canned fruits and vegetables
- published books (This one bothers me a little, but maybe it reflects the fact that books have become wonderfully cheap; in fact, the book in your hand probably cost about as much as twenty-four twelve-ounce bottles of cheap beer or two six-packs of better stuff.)
- paints, varnishes and shellacs, appropriate again because some of the factories are almost interchangeable
- household appliances

Cost

When you buy a case of canned beer in a retail outlet, here's where each dollar of your money goes. The can and its carrier cost about twenty-six cents, and filling it cost two and a half cents more. All the ingredients and labor cost nine cents. Marketing gets six cents; all those heart-warming commercials that stretch the seventh inning stretch have to be paid for somehow. A little over two cents goes to depreciation and interest and four cents is the brewer's profit. Shipping cost a penny and a half and taxes were around thirty cents. (I'm being vague about the taxes—the actual figure varies a lot depending on where you live.)

All told, your beer dollar cost the wholesaler sixty-six cents. If there's a retailer involved, she shelled out eighty-one cents before you handed over your dollar.

If you drink an import, the current US tariff on beer is thirteen and a half cents a case. Until now, the brewing industry hasn't lobbied for an increase. With beer sales flat and the large brewers trying their hand at mock-premium beers, the situation may change.

Now these numbers only apply to cans purchased at a retail outlet like a supermarket. If you buy returnable bottles at the same source, your dollar buys 10 percent more beer and less of your money goes to the package. The returnable package takes a dime from your buck and shipping is almost a quarter. Returnables are much cheaper than cans because they have a life expectancy of ten refills; they're also heavier and more fragile, so it costs more to truck them around. It's possible that cans are what made it feasible for mega-brewers to ship their product over long distances and compete with local brewers. It's also possible that one effect of a return to reusable bottles will be a reversal of this trend.

Exports

Many people are surprised to find out that we Americans export any beer at all. How much beer could we sell overseas? The real answer to the question is "not much," even when you consider that American beers are a status symbol in East Asia and supported by aggressive marketing in Canada. In fact we sell about 2,500,000 barrels of beer, most of it to Japan and Canada. Exports represent about 1 per cent of our total national production.

The future of American exports in these markets and in the third world as well probably relies on licensing agreements. With these commercial alliances, a foreign company licenses its recipe and trademarks to another to produce its beer in the domestic market. Heineken has licensed breweries in almost twenty countries and has used licensing as a major strategy in its growth. In Japan, this is a way for foreign companies to enter Japan's closed and complicated distribution system. Guinness has overseas licenses and was even produced in the US under license for a while.

Discussion Questions

1. If religious organizations were encouraged, by tax laws, let's say, to make beer, would American beer be better than it is?
2. It doesn't cost much money for a bar to become a beer bar: a case each of six to ten really interesting beers. How many beer-loving customers do you think it would take for your local tavern to become your local beer temple?
3. If you were going to have a contract-brewed beer made, what would it taste like? What would you call it? No, what would you really call it?

Afterword

Beer is worth your attention for at least five reasons.

Because it's our history. Drinking beer didn't make us human, but it made us civilized. Beer is no longer the pivotal cultural object that it used to be, but the connections between this drink and our civilization run deep. To know nothing about beer is to know less about ourselves.

Because beer can be beautiful. I choose the word "beautiful" consciously. I mean that beer can be something that's worth a moment of aesthetic appreciation as in "damn, that's a good glass of beer." That's not the same as saying that beer is art; the Grand Canyon isn't art either, but we don't begrudge ourselves the opportunity to enjoy its beauty.

Because beer offers lots of opportunities for connoisseur- and craftsmanship. You can enjoy the pleasure of developing a refined and knowledgeable palate. You may also want to revel in the satisfaction of having produced something wonderful in your own little kitchen-turned-brew house.

Because beer is a pivotal part of a social and cultural movement toward more conscious eating and drinking. It's exciting to be involved with good beer right now, and the people who are involved in it tend to be pretty interesting too.

Because it represents a chance to shut up and pay attention to the world around us. Aren't you tired of listening to all that noise in our heads, that blah, blah, blah of self-talking, of fantasizing sex and plotting revenge and replaying past mistakes? Beer is one of the things that invites us to connect with the world outside in a genuine way. Good beer leads us *Back to the Present*. Think of it as yoga with 6 percent alcohol thrown in.

Appendix A

Beer Tourism

The question is not how long beer tourism has been going on. The right question is, how long have people admitted that the real reason for their travels is to drink great beer in pleasant places?

Belgium

Until recently, if Americans thought about beer quality at all, they thought about German beers. Their thoughts may not have been especially clear or accurate, but German imports plainly held pride of place.

In the last few years, as beer has become more popular, our view of beer's homeland has broadened somewhat. One of the happiest inclusions has been Belgium. The Belgians drink just a bit more than we do—120 liters a year as against 90, but they drink a great deal better.

Part of their good fortune lies in the diversity of their brewing industry. Belgium supports more than 100 breweries, many of them small, quirky enterprises that sell most of their beer within walking distance of the brew house. There are about 600 different beers available at any one time and maybe 700 during the course of a year. This is in a country with fewer than 10 million people.

Now just in case you're not stunned by the implications of these numbers, let me stun you myself. At the same rate of beer enthusiasm, Philadelphia would have seventeen breweries (it has four) and 120 brands of strictly local beer. There would be thirty breweries in Brooklyn, 3000 in the USA. What's more, all this hoppy exuberance is packed into a country that's just a little bit bigger than Maryland.

It's difficult to characterize Belgian beer by anything except its exuberant diversity and the unrelenting connoisseurship of the Belgians. At any meeting of beer mavens, there is a considerable body of opinion in favor of the notion that the next generation of great beer making in the United States will be more closely modeled on Belgian beers than on German or English ones. As a harbinger of the next generation, a Belgian beer maker named Pierre Celis briefly operated a brewery in Austin, Texas.

For more information about Belgian beer tourism, go to **http://www.shortcourse in beer.com/tourism**

Austria

If you're going to Austria to eat and drink, chances are that you've got wine on your mind. As a wine destination, Austria has it all: autochthonous varieties, perfect winemaking, gaspingly beautiful scenery, elegant cities, tiny independent wineries and very reasonable prices. The same spirit illuminates the brewing scene and Austrians are the world's fifth most enthusiastic beer drinkers: they down 109 liters per head per year. The styles are a combination of German pilsner and international innovation. You can tour a monastic brewery, listen to Gregorian chant and then head back to Vienna to have a sunset beer in a chic brewpub. Be sure to check out the Mühlviertel, between the Danube and the Bohemian Forest. This region includes Austria's only monastery brewery in Schlägel Abbey; the country's oldest brewery, the Gutsbrauhof in St. Martin; the long-established Municipal Braucommune in Freistadt; and countless castle breweries, palace breweries and other small breweries. And of course, it's a short train ride to the original Budweiser brewery in Budvar, Czech Republic.

Germany

The Germans seem to have figured out just how much value that foreign beer lovers can add to their tourist economy. You can follow the Bamberg Brewery Trail for instance, following the tasting notes in that city's own brochure. Or you can set out on your own, planning your trip around small breweries with their own guesthouses.

Beer bath at a spa in Bavaria.

These Brauereigasthoefen are mostly concentrated in the pictur-
esque southern part of the country. Accommodations are always
comfortable although not necessarily luxurious, and the breweries
are often minor works of art. I can personally recommend the Gast-
hof at the Ayinger brewery in Aying, Bavaria, and the glorious little
brewpub attached to it. By the way, don't be startled by the frequent
display of the six-pointed Star of David. In Bavaria—indeed in most
of Europe—it's also a symbol of the brewers' art which the good
king was supposed to have practiced.

For more information on beer tourism, go to:

http://www.shortcourseinbeer.com/tourism

UK

Unfortunately, the friendly pub on the town square with lots of
craft-brewed beer is more a figment than a fact. The individuality of

Main street outside of Aying brewery in Bavaria.

UK pubs has suffered over the years: many are part of multi-outlet chains and others are "tied" to individual breweries. The unfortunate result is that if you walk into a pub at random, you'll be likely to find the same bland industrial beer that you crossed the pond to get away from.

There is lots of good beer still to be found, but you need local knowledge. The best source—unless you have kin in the kingdom—is CAMRA's real beer guide. You can order it online before you go or download a PDF version.

USA

There's probably no town that's more beer-friendly than Philadelphia, home to Monk's Cafe, the now-venerable Belgian beer bar that got the good beer revolution going, and lots of ex-

A street in the comfortable brewing town of Aying, Bavaria.

citing newcomers like Grace Tavern, Eulogy and the quaintly named Devil's Den. The Belgian influence remains strong in this city, with half a dozen places specializing in Belgian styles, although local beer guide Don Russell says that both tradition and diversity drive the scene. On the other coast, Portland is heavily beered with an emphasis on hoppy British styles, stouts and porters. In both cities, look for exciting annual beer festivals. For up-to-the-minute travel advice on planning a beer trip, go to

http://www.shortcourseinbeer.com/travel

By the way, if you're looking for beer-friendly countries, here's the per-capita list, compiled by Kirin Brewing of Japan:

Rank	Rank in 2003	Country	Per capita volume			Total consumption (1,000 kL)
			Consump-tion (L)	Number of bottles in standard size 633-mL bottles	Year-on-year increase (bottles)	
1	1	Czech Republic	156.9	247.9	-3.2	1,878
2	2	Ireland	131.1	207.1	-7.1	521
3	3	Germany	115.8	182.9	-3.2	9,555
4	4	Australia	109.9	173.6	-7.6	1,678
5	5	Austria	108.3	171.1	-3.6	885
6	6	UK	99.0	156.4	-3.6	5,920
7	8	Belgium	93.0	146.9	-4.7	970
8	7	Denmark	89.9	142.0	-9.8	486
9	16	Finland	85.0	134.3	11.7	437
10	10	Luxemburg	84.4	133.3	-0.5	39
11	9	Slovakia	84.1	132.9	-8.5	456
12	12	Spain	83.8	132.4	0.9	3,376
13	13	US	81.6	128.9	-0.3	23,974
14	11	Croatia	81.2	128.3	-4.3	365
15	14	Netherlands	79.0	124.8	-2.7	1,269
16	15	New Zealand	77.0	121.6	-1.9	313
17	17	Hungary	75.3	119.0	2.8	755
18	18	Poland	69.1	109.2	-2.7	2,670
19	19	Canada	68.3	107.9	-0.2	2,183
20	22	Portugal	59.6	94.2	3.6	627
21	26	Bulgaria	59.5	94.0	4.4	448
22	23	South Africa	59.2	93.5	3.0	2,530
23	29	Russia	58.9	93.0	9.3	8,450
24	21	Venezuela	58.6	92.6	0.0	1,525
25	24	Romania	58.2	91.9	1.4	1,302
26	25	Cyprus	58.1	91.8	1.7	45

27	20	Switzerland	57.3	90.5	-2.2	426
28	27	Gabon	55.8	88.2	-0.9	76
29	32	Norway	55.5	87.7	8.7	249
30	30	Mexico	51.8	81.8	0.6	5,435
31	28	Sweden	51.5	81.4	-3.9	464
32	31	Japan	51.3	81.0	0.6	6,549
33	33	Brazil	47.6	75.2	1.3	8,450
34	34	South Korea	38.5	60.8	0.0	1,897
35	36	Colombia	36.8	58.1	0.3	1,658
Reference		China	22.1	34.9	3.8	28,640

Appendix B

John Barleycorn by Robert Burns, 1732

There was three kings into the east,
Three kings both great and high,
And they hae sworn a solemn oath
John Barleycorn should die.

They took a plough and plough'd him down,
Put clods upon his head,
And they hae sworn a solemn oath
John Barleycorn was dead.

But the cheerful Spring came kindly on,
And show'rs began to fall;
John Barleycorn got up again,
And sore surpris'd them all.

The sultry suns of Summer came,
And he grew thick and strong;
His head weel arm'd wi' pointed spears,
That no one should him wrong.

The sober Autumn enter'd mild,
When he grew wan and pale;
His bending joints and drooping head
Show'd he began to fail.

His colour sicken'd more and more,
He faded into age;
And then his enemies began

To show their deadly rage.

They've taen a weapon, long and sharp,
And cut him by the knee;
Then tied him fast upon a cart,
Like a rogue for forgerie.

They laid him down upon his back,
And cudgell'd him full sore;
They hung him up before the storm,
And turn'd him o'er and o'er.

They laid him out upon the floor,
To work him further woe;
And still, as signs of life appear'd,
They toss'd him to and fro.

They wasted, o'er a scorching flame,
The marrow of his bones;
But a miller us'd him worst of all,
For he crush'd him between two stones.

And they hae taen his very heart's blood,
And drank it round and round;
And still the more and more they drank,
Their joy did more abound.

John Barleycorn was a hero bold,
Of noble enterprise;
For if you do but taste his blood,
'Twill make your courage rise.

'Twill make a man forget his woe;

'Twill heighten all his joy;
'Twill make the widow's heart to sing,
Tho' the tear were in her eye.

Then let us toast John Barleycorn,
Each man a glass in hand;
And may his great posterity
Ne'er fail in old Scotland!

Appendix C:

The Reinheitsgebot

The Reinheitsgebot is sometimes reverentially spoken of as the German Beer Purity Law. This, like some other recent German uses of the word "purity" is a bit inappropriate. In fact the Bavarian law of 1516 is about price limits, recipes and ingredients. The section that's often cited reads:

> We would especially like that throughout our cities, markets, and in our countryside, no beer be brewed with any ingredients other than barley, hops and water.

The unification of Western Europe's economies in 1992 has forced the Germans to give up the Reinheitsgebot in the same spirit that other nations had to give up other standards that excluded their neighbors' produce.

The demise of this law, which we may now think of as the Reinheitsge-bye-bye, has met with a mixed reaction from the beer community. Aside from pure malty nostalgia, the law was esteemed for preventing the sort of flavorless degeneracy that befell American beer. No law could enforce quality, but this law insured at least a minimum standard of ingredients and helped create an atmosphere in which quality was expected. With the law gone, price competition will lead some brewers and force some others into using adjuncts in place of malt. The flood of cheaper foreign beers is sure to call the question.

Other observers note that Reinheitsgebot deprived Germans of Trappist ales, lambics, stouts and fruit beers. Some have noted that the famous German wheat beers are violations of the law. They have pointed out that a law from such a different era (it was written before there was knowledge of yeast) needs reconsideration simply because it's so foreign to our times. They also point to the fact that beers for export do not conform; if a little rice or corn is all right for foreigners, what could be the tragic outcome of offering such beer to Germans? Some writers have even attributed the German prohibition of home brewing to some vague umbra of Reinheitsgebot falling across the land.

In all, the end of the single-recipe era will probably create a wave of cheaper beers in Germany. How deeply those beers will penetrate a prosperous market used to good beer remains to be seen. Chances are that non-German immigrants will be the biggest consumers. The new climate is sure to promote a new era of German beer advertising as brewers try to explain why the newer beers are better.

Voluntary adherence to the Reinheitsgebot will probably develop into a major marketing tool for native brewers, but look for some of them to develop 'lighter' lines of adjunct-brewed beer and to market them with vigorous misdirection.

The happiest possibilities involve the possible development of new German beer styles, particularly in the western part of the country. Germany is still a country with a lot of small breweries and brewpubs. Even if the domestic market proves too conservative for the innovators, there is a ready foreign market for German beer. Even with Germany's tiny breweries, mixed image and lack of marketing experience in America, Germans are the fourth largest importers of beer to the US. As the natives of Bordeaux and Oporto will tell you, there is nothing like a band of middle-class foreign enthusiasts to stimulate the development of a whole new style of drink.

Appendix D

Recommended Reading

Homebrewing

There are probably three books that are genuinely helpful for the beginning homebrewer. Which one is right for you depends on how you approach techniques of dealing with things in the physical world.

The Complete Joy of Homebrewing by Charlie Papazian
> If the idea of doing anything physical scares the bejabbers out of you, look for *The Complete Joy of Homebrewing*. This is a very simple, slow and reassuring book. The author sounds like the friendliest, least intimidating guy in the world. The style is very chummy in a post-frathouse kind of way that some people find very difficult to read and that others find relaxing. In this book you may see the ancestor of the Complete Dummies series. I believe that Papazian, who has made a career of coaching homebrewers, has been published on the topic for thirty years or so.

How to Brew: Everything You Need To Know To Brew Beer Right The First Time by John J. Palmer
> A nicely written, personal session with a very thoughtful brewer. An excellent second brewing book and a great night-stand companion for the intermediate or advanced brewer. Of all the authors who talk about homebrewing, John J. Palmer is by far the best writer. His prose is witty, entertaining and relentlessly focused on clarifying the complexities and celebrating the simplicities of the small-scale brewing of beer.

If you love fundamentals, then Palmer's is the book for you. There are dozens of complications lurking in Palmer's world of brewing and a host of precautions and gadgets for avoiding them. The author is not a negative soul; on the contrary, he seems like a guy who just wants to get to the bottom of things. How to Brew is also the book for those who are themselves curious about fundamentals: the hard science of brewing is to be found here.

The Happy Brewer, Wilf Newsom
Although this book is copyrighted in 1978, it reflects a style and a way of thinking about brewing that reflects Britain in the years after the war. There's a sort of chirpy cheerfulness about Newsom's discussion that's only a turn or two away from a Monty Python skit. There are also frequent references to matters of economy: homebrewing can save you money and it's really not that much of a bother.

On the other hand, in some ways Newsom's discussion is more advanced than that of modern brew books. He has to deal with waters of wildly varying hardness and so his discussion is quite sophisticated. He describes yeast cultures and various microscopic conditions of beer, and his chapter on filtering and fining is more than adequate.

Newsom's recipes are instructive; sugar and extract abounds and mashing temperatures, when required, are low. In all, this is a jolly little book with a few surprising lessons, a lovely historic item for the homebrewer and a great gift.

The Complete Handbook of Home Brewing by David G. Miller
If you're the sort of person who likes the idea of baking his own bread or wiring her own lamp, then probably this book, *The Complete Handbook*, is right for you. The information is straightforward and well organized, and the author allows for

the fact that sometimes you want to make it fast and simple and other times you may want to linger over the details. There's a separate book of recipes ordered by beer style and also by degree of difficulty. I still have notes on recipes that I brewed two decades ago that are just marked: Miller, p55.

Radical Brewing by Randy Mosher

The Compleat Meadmaker by Ken Schramm

Beer Styles

The New World Guide to Beer by Michael Jackson
This was one of the books that supported the craft beer movement when it first got started. It is a book whose graphic standards give its subject the respect that it deserves.

Michael Jackson was the first beer journalist, and his writing is exceptional, both terse and witty. Much of the information on particular beers is out of date, but that doesn't seem to diminish this book's charm.

Brew Like a Monk: Trappist, Abbey, and Strong Belgian Ales and How to Brew Them by Stan Hieronymus
Imagine that you, an experienced homebrewer, got to gather around a fire with some folks who had years of experience brewing versions of your favorite beer style. It would be hard to have a bad time, harder still not to come away a better brewer for it.

This friendly, if somewhat disorderly book, is just that conversation. I love the complexity and depth of Belgian strong beers. Occasionally, by dumb luck, I've brewed one. Other times, my efforts have been dull, or over-concentrated or just odd.

In these conversations, we get some clarity about yeast, malt, fermenters, temperature control and bottling. I think the odds in my favor just went up. This is a book to mine for insights.

Farmhouse Ales: Culture and Craftsmanship in the Belgian Tradition by Phil Markowski

These are some of my favorite beers: I like to brew them and I like to drink them. This is an excellent book that has helped improve my beer. It's also alerted me to the tyranny of the idea of "beer styles." Not every family of beers can be described by referring to the standard beer judge criteria: sometimes history and culture are just more important.

Well-written and fun to read, this is one of the best books for the advanced homebrewer.

Classic Stout and Porter by Roger Protz

Roger Protz's prose is lean and intelligent without many of the adolescent flourishes that plague beer writing. He also seems to be a fellow who's willing to consult primary sources rather than just pass on the folklore and fakelore of other beer writers. This good, short history clears away a lot of the silliness that surrounds the story of porter and stout. Protz's technical knowledge of the brewing process illuminates both the history that comprises the first ninety-six pages and the guide to beers that makes up most of the rest. The illustrations are generous, appropriate and well reproduced. Indispensable for lovers of this delightful style of beer.

Wild Brews: Beer Beyond the Influence of Brewer's Yeast by Jeffrey Sparrow

This is one of a series of books about Belgian beer that takes a look at style that seems to have survived from the past. *Wild*

Brews is a discussion of beers that are fermented with wild yeasts and with (gasp!) bacteria.

Most beer lovers have had an encounter with these beers: they are shocking, original and, to our tastes, most un-beer–like. They tend to be either distinctly sour or sweet and sour. Their effect in the mouth is thirst quenching in the manner of a tart lemonade, and they are often surprisingly aromatic.

Jeff Sparrow has provided an introduction to the history and brewing techniques of these beers that seems to grow out of a deep knowledge of the biochemistry involved and a major involvement in the Belgian brewing community. As a beer lover, I find this book to be a revelation, and it has led me back to some beers that I haven't tasted in years.

As a brewer, it scares the daylights out of me. Letting organisms like pediococcus and brettanomyces loose in your brew house or kitchen is risky. Outcomes with these organisms are always uncertain and aging can involve super-attenuation and unusual mouth-feel.

Beer Business

Ambitious Brew: The Story of American Beer by Maureen Ogle
This is a business history of brewing in America. What is especially fascinating is the story of the rise of the great brewing families and the impact of Prohibition. Ogle is willing to tackle the complex and fragmented story of the rise of microbreweries and the gradual absorption of the industrial giants by multi-national corporations.

In a day when the largest American-owned brewery is the former micro, Sam Adams, *Ambitious Brew* is the perfect book to see how it happened.

Beer School: Bottling Success at the Brooklyn Brewery by Steve

Hindy and Tom Potter

It's sad that Brooklyn, which once brewed more beer than Milwaukee, saw the last of its big breweries close in 1976. This was the city that thumbed its nose at Prohibition and boasted more saloons than churches. Twenty years later, Brooklyn Brewery produced a premium craft-brewed beer. This is the story of the group of pioneers who made it possible. It also happens to be an extraordinarily well-written business biography.

Brewing Up a Business: Adventures in Entrepreneurship from the Founder of Dogfish Head Craft Brewery by Sam Calagione

This is more a reminiscence than a biography of a business, but Calagione is charming and his beer is delicious. If you like the brew, you'll love the book.

Index

Photo: Earth Bread + Brewery

ABOUT
Lynn Hoffman

Lynn Hoffman is an award-winning writer, executive chef, much-exhibited photographer and a lecturer on fine wines and food history. Among his published works are *The Bachelor's Cat*, *The New Short Course in Wine* and *Bang Bang*. He was chef-professor at a major culinary program for fifteen years.

Cooked in LA ■ Paul Cook

How does a successful young man from a "good" home hit bottom and risk losing it all? *Cooked In La* shows how a popular, middle-class young man with a bright future in radio and television is nearly destroyed by a voracious appetite for drugs and alcohol.

Non Fiction/Self-Help & Recovery | US$ 24.95
Pages 304 | Cloth 5.5" x 8.5"
ISBN 978-1-60164-193-9

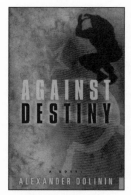

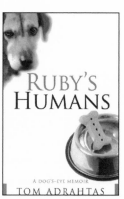

Against Destiny
■ Alexander Dolinin

A story of courage and determination in the face of the impossible. The dilemma of the unjustly condemned: Die in slavery or die fighting for your freedom.

Fiction | US$ 24.95
Pages 448 | Cloth 5.5" x 8.5"
ISBN 978-1-60164-173-1

Let the Shadows Fall Behind You
■ Kathy-Diane Leveille

The disappearance of her lover turns a young woman's world upside down and leads to shocking revelations of her past. This enigmatic novel is about connections and relationships, memory and reality.

Fiction | US$ 22.95
Pages 288 | Cloth 5.5" x 8.5"
ISBN 978-1-60164-167-0

Ruby's Humans
■ Tom Adrahtas

No other book tells a story of abuse, neglect, escape, recovery and love with such humor and poignancy, in the uniquely perceptive words of a dog. Anyone who's ever loved a dog will love Ruby's sassy take on human foibles and manners.

Non Fiction | US$ 19.95
Pages 192 | Cloth 5.5" x 8.5"
ISBN 978-1-60164-188-5

The Unbreakable Child ■ Kim Michele Richardson

Starved, beaten and abused for nearly a decade, orphan Kimmi learned that evil can wear a nun's habit. A story not just of a survivor but of a rare spirit who simply would not be broken.

Non Fiction/True Crime I US$ 24.95
Pages 256 I Cloth 5.5" x 8.5"
ISBN 978-1-60164-163-2

Save the Whales Please
■ Konrad Karl Gatien & Sreescanda

Japanese threats and backroom deals cause the slaughter of more whales than ever. The first lady risks everything—her life, her position, her marriage—to save the whales.

Fiction I US$ 24.95
Pages 432 I Cloth 5.5" x 8.5"
ISBN 978-1-60164-165-6

Screenshot
■ John Darrin

Could you resist the lure of evil that lurks in the anonymous power of the Internet? Every week, a mad entrepreneur presents an execution, the live, real-time murder of someone who probably deserves it. *Screenshot*: a techno-thriller with a provocative premise.

Fiction I US$ 24.95
Pages 416 I Cloth 5.5" x 8.5"
ISBN 978-1-60164-168-7

KÜNATI

Kunati Book Titles

•••••••••••••••••••••••••••••••••

Provocative. Bold. Controversial.

Touchstone Tarot ■ Kat Black

Internationally renowned tarot designer Kat Black, whose *Golden Tarot* remains one of the most popular and critically acclaimed tarot decks on the market, has created this unique new deck. In *Touchstone Tarot*, Kat Black uses Baroque masterpieces as the basis for her sumptuous and sensual collaged portraits. Intuitive and easy to read, this deck is for readers at every level of experience. This deluxe set, with gold gilt edges and sturdy hinged box includes a straightforward companion book with card explanations and sample readings.

Non Fiction/New Age I US$ 32.95 I Tarot box set with 200-page booklet I Cards and booklet 3.5" x 5" ISBN 978-1-60164-190-8

Sleepers Awake
■ Patrick McNulty

Monstrous creatures invade our world in this dark fantasy in which death is but a door to another room of one's life.

Fiction I US$ 22.95 Pages 320 I Cloth 5.5" x 8.5" ISBN 978-1-60164-166-3

The Nation's Highest Honor
■ James Gaitis

Like Kosinski's classic *Being There*, *The Nation's Highest Honor* demonstrates the dangerous truth that incompetence is no obstacle to making a profound difference in the world.

Fiction I US$ 22.95 Pages 256 I Cloth 5.5" x 8.5" ISBN 978-1-60164-172-4

The Woman Who Would Be Pharaoh
■ William Klein

Shadowy figures from Egypt's fabulous past glow with color and authenticity. Tragic love story weaves a rich tapestry of history, mystery, regicide and incest.

Fiction/Historic I US$ 24.95 Pages 304 I Cloth 5.5" x 8.5" ISBN 978-1-60164-189-2

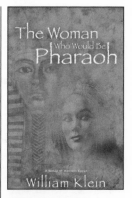